SHOCK AND ALARM

CreateSpace titles may be purchased in bulk for educational, business, fundraising, or sales promotional use. For information, please email ShockAndAlarm@ EducationTransfer.com.

ISBN: 1481202960
ISBN 13: 9781481202961
Library of Congress Control Number: 2012923432
CreateSpace Independent Publishing Platform
North Charleston, South Carolina

Library of Congress Cataloging-in-Publication Data

Iwanicki, Hugh & Bailey, Dave
Includes bibliographical references and Glossary
    1. Iraq. 2. Jordan. 3. Kuwait. 4. Islamic Law – Social aspects.
    5. Christians – Legal status, evangelism, conversion, etc. (Islamic law).
    6. Islam – Controversial literature. I. Title.

Printed in the United States of America

SHOCK★K
AND *ALARM*

What it was *really* like at the U.S. Embassy in Iraq

By Hugh Iwanicki
with Dave Bailey

CreateSpace

This book is dedicated to the Christians and other religious minorities in Iraq who suffer egregious persecution and are being harassed out of their own country. We hope that this book shines a light upon their suffering, and will ultimately help them receive comfort and safety.

Disclaimer

The opinions and characterizations in this book are those of the authors, and do not necessarily represent official positions of the United States Government. Some individuals in this book have granted permission to use their real names. The names and personal information of all other individuals have been changed to conceal their identities. In these cases, any resemblance to real persons, living or dead, is purely coincidental.

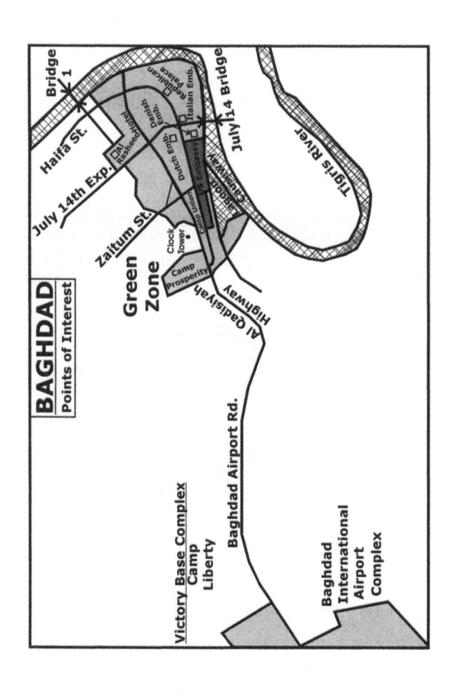

BAGHDAD
Points of Interest

Bridge 1

Haifa St.

July 14th Exp.

Al Rasheed Hotel

Danish Emb.

Dutch Emb.

Republican Palace

Italian Emb.

US Embassy

July 14 Bridge

14th July Causeway

Zaitum St.

Green Zone

Clock Tower

Camp Union

Camp Prosperity

Al Qadisiyah Highway

Tigris River

Baghdad Airport Rd.

Victory Base Complex
Camp Liberty

Baghdad International Airport Complex

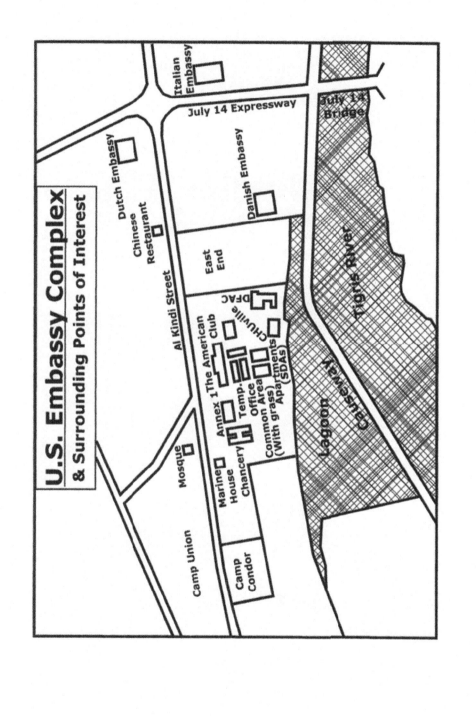

U.S. Embassy Complex

& Surrounding Points of Interest

Italian Embassy

July 14 Expressway

July 14 Bridge

Dutch Embassy

Chinese Restaurant

Danish Embassy

Al Kindi Street

East End

Tigris River

DFAC

Chuville

Common Area (With grass)

Apartments (SDAs)

Lagoon

Causeway

The American Club

Annex 1

Temp. Office

Marine House

Chancery

Mosque

Camp Union

Camp Condor

Contents

Preface and Acknowledgements

This book began with a friendship, and without that friendship it never would have happened.

When Hugh launched upon his tour of Iraq as a Performance Auditor with the Department of State, Office of Inspector General, his long-time friend Dave encouraged him to keep a log of his experiences so that Hugh could share them with his family, church members, and other friends. Later, as Hugh's dispatches began arriving from Iraq, Dave would edit them into journal entries for others to read and Hugh would broadcast them.

These journal entries were received enthusiastically by their audiences because they helped readers get a grip on a new era the United States finds itself in – one that is deeply intertwined with a potentially hostile Islamic world. We perceived a desire among friends and family to have an eye-witness account of that world, particularly from someone they knew and could trust.

While most Americans realize that the September 11 attacks changed history forever, few truly understand the culture out of which those attacks arose. While modern Western culture has had its share of atrocities committed by lone wolves, cults, and gangs, an attack of the scale of 9/11, heavily funded and coordinated by a network of ideological fanatics, remains incomprehensible to most people. We intended to use these journal entries to help others understand the cultural ocean in which Islamic terrorism swims, and how it contrasts with our own.

As Hugh finished his time in Iraq, we realized that his journal entries were the beginnings of a book that any Westerner could appreciate. To write that book, we identified narrative gaps and sections that needed additional context and then assembled the entries into a single coherent stream of thoughts and events.

Along the way, friends from the Embassy added their own perspectives and colorful details. We are especially grateful to Richard Pemberton, Herb Brown, and Robin Rowan, whose perspectives added depth and robustness to Hugh's recollections.

In addition, friends and family members reviewed the text to make sure it had enough detail and background information to make sense to anyone. Our deepest gratitude goes to Marta Strada, Rev. Chris Looker, Frieda and Charles Bailey, Rock Peters, Bob Petrusak, and Joe and Rosanne Giarracco for their feedback. We believe that their labors have produced a book that others will be able to read with ease.

We also want to thank our wives, Ping and Linda, for their enduring patience while we often disappeared for hours to work on the manuscript or discuss revisions. The lonely hours they spent while we were glued to our computer monitors and phones were sacrifices we deeply appreciate.

We hope you'll find that this book makes the Islamic world, as well as life at a U.S. Embassy during wartime, more comprehensible. We also hope that it gives you a more human understanding of the sacrifices that members of the International Coalition, from the soldiers in remote outposts, to the embassy staff, to the people who fix the plumbing and wash dishes, endure to keep our country safe. Most importantly, we hope that this book conveys the magnitude of what is at stake in the Middle East. It is not just the future of Iraq that is being written; it is our own as well.

– Hugh Iwanicki and Dave Bailey, March 19, 2011

Abbreviations

ABPO: American Based Presbyterian Organization
ACE: Army Corps of Engineers
CHU: Containerized Housing Unit, also known as a hooch
DCM: Deputy Chief of Mission
DFAC: Dining FACility
DOD: Department of Defense
FOB: Forward Operating Base
FSO: Foreign Service Officer
GAO: Government Accountability Office
IED: Improvised Explosive Device
IG: Inspector General
INL: International Narcotics and Law enforcement (a bureau of the U.S. State Dept.)
ITAO: Iraq Transition and Assistance Office
IZ: International Zone, also known as the Green Zone
KBR: Kellogg, Brown, & Root; formerly a division of Halliburton
LGBT: Lesbian, Gay, Bisexual, Transgender
MBB: Muslim By Birth or Muslim Before Believing (describes a Christian who was previously Muslim)
MERO: Middle East Regional Office
NEC: New Embassy Compound
OIG: Office of the Inspector General
PAE: Pacific Architects and Engineers
PCUSA: Presbyterian Church USA
PPE: Personal Protective Equipment
R&R: Rest and Relaxation
REO: Regional Embassy Office
RSO: Regional Security Officer
SDA: Single Diplomat Accommodation
SUV: Sport-Utility Vehicle
SIGIR: Special Inspector General for Iraq Reconstruction
TCN: Third Country National (in the context of this book, a person at the U.S. Embassy in Iraq who is from neither the U.S. nor Iraq)

Prologue

The Embassy Edition of
Worst Case Scenario

If a person working for the U.S. Embassy in Iraq tried to tell his or her friends what it was like there, one way would be to say, "Have you ever heard of the survival game called Worst Case Scenario? Well, it's kind of like that, except that it's not a game. And sometimes you don't survive, because the questions don't have answers."

During my time in Iraq, I picked up many valuable real-life skills, including:

- How to shoot any of a wide variety of weapons after recovering it from a dead body
- How to drive a vehicle when someone is trying to kill you
- How to drive a vehicle in typical Middle Eastern traffic (see above)
- First aid for a dismembered hand
- What to do when you hear "INCOMING! INCOMING! INCOMING!"
- How a bunker can save your life
- How to survive a week-long dust storm
- How to avoid getting killed if you're a Muslim
- How to avoid getting killed if you're *not* a Muslim

- How to prevent a long-distance marriage from ending in divorce
- How to avoid going crazy
- How to tap into an unlimited supply of free beer

If you're a fan of Worst Case Scenario, the questions that these how-to's raise should produce an instinctive desire to flip cards for answers. You can do this by flipping the pages of this book. However, the goal of this book is not simply to provide isolated answers to questions. To really understand the questions, it helps to learn about the scenarios where they arose.

The first question you may ask is, "What could lead a person to work for the U.S. Embassy in Iraq?" This memoir will answer that question and then deal with the others as I encountered them over the ensuing months.

Unfortunately, this book also raises real-life questions that have no easy answers. What's more, these questions are not relegated to a remote part of the world; instead they are confronting us with escalating urgency here in the United States. Years after a triumphal campaign of "Shock and Awe" in Iraq, we find ourselves shocked and *alarmed* at the unanticipated effects that press upon us ever-closer to home.

I hope you'll join me on this journey, which leads to a search for answers to our own worst-case scenarios here in the United States.

Joining Up

October to November 2008

When I entered the accounting profession and became a CPA, I expected a career of regular hours and professionalism. I pictured the most demanding stresses as late-night deadlines and believed that my strangest adventure might be something like climbing into a grain silo to inspect an inventory. However, in the manner of an aspiring veterinary student told to don a long glove and inspect a cow's colon, I have learned how far reality can veer from expectation. This is a tale of the most eye-opening audit assignment I've ever had.

For six years, I consulted with companies in manufacturing, finance, and government contracting. However the economic downturn of 2008 left me, like many other Americans, "on the bench," wondering what my next assignment would be. The consulting company that employed me was running out of engagements, so I knew that it was time to explore new opportunities. After a few months passed, a friend told me about an advertisement he saw in the Washington Post for auditors at the U.S. Embassy in Iraq. After reading its description I thought, "Why not? The pay is good, and after six years of the 8 to 5 routine I could use some excitement."

CPAs are not known for being adventurous, but I had already departed from the beaten path once before, back in 1998 when I was pursuing my

MBA. For six months I lived in Taiwan to help a local church establish an English school as an outreach program for its community. During that time I studied Chinese and developed an appreciation for China's proud and ancient civilization. It proved to be an enlightening and rewarding experience and, among other benefits, it ultimately led to my marriage. Later, while working in Delaware, I fell in love with a Chinese graduate student at the University of Delaware nicknamed Ping. A few years later we married and moved to northern Virginia. Given my pleasant trip down a road less traveled, I had no fear of venturing out again.

From the perspective of learning about the Middle East, this auditing position looked like an exceptional opportunity to visit a proud and ancient land. I would also no longer be a mere bean-counter, but instead would be a kind of pioneer, helping to cultivate democracy where formerly there had only been ruthless dictatorship. This was exciting!

At the time, Ping and I had been married for four years and were pleasantly settled into a comfortable lifestyle in suburban Washington, DC. Therefore I should have realized that Ping would not be as thrilled with my far-flung career aspiration as I was.

When I shared my plan to work for a year in Iraq, her response was, "What?! You could get killed!" However, as I explained the long-term benefits of a job with the federal government, and the increased compensation for working in Iraq, she reluctantly agreed to my grand experiment.

At about the same time, the Presbyterian Church we attended hosted a presentation called *Rumi Returning*. It included a movie based on the life story and Islamic teachings of an ancient Sufi poet named Jalal ad-Din Muhammad Rumi.[1]

The presenter said that he had been deeply impressed by the "message of Rumi," and told our packed church that "the very essence of Islam is peace." The presentation, with its recitations of Rumi's poetry, was beautiful, but for me there was a disconnect between the movie's utopian message and the realities I read about every day, of violence, poverty, and chaos in the Islamic world. However, this non-sequitur was completely ignored by the presenter and no one in the audience was impolite enough to ask about it. Still, I wondered...

---

1   Rumi was a 13th Century Persian IslamicSufi poet. See http://en.wikipedia.org/wiki/Rumi .

Three weeks after applying to the U.S. Department of State for the Iraq position, I was interviewed and soon received an attractive tentative offer. Once they cleared me, I was hired.

This was the chance of a lifetime – a lucrative opportunity to travel the world and work for a U.S. embassy. What a resume builder!

There was another attraction as well. I hoped that this would also be an opportunity to learn something about this "religion of peace" that *Rumi Returning* praised so glowingly. Perhaps this trip could answer some of the questions that the presentation never addressed.

My adventure began in October of 2008 when I reported for induction to the State Department's Office of the Inspector General (OIG) Middle East Regional Office (MERO) in Rosslyn, Virginia. It started with an employee orientation similar to the others I've had, with two exceptions: (1) a two-week course on Iraqi culture and the Arabic language, and (2) a one-week "Crash and Bang" course for all personnel bound for Iraq or Afghanistan, provided at a former racetrack in the autumn-colored hills of West Virginia. While the course on Iraqi culture and the Arabic language was academic, the "Crash and Bang" course was a dose of bone-crunching reality.

The "Crash" portion of this course was a training program in defensive driving. Its goal was to teach us how to avoid kidnappings while operating in a "stressful environment."

It turned out that "stressful environment" meant that the instructors played bad guys who blocked our vehicles with their own while shooting at us with *very* realistic blanks. It also meant something even more stressful. We had to learn to ram *their* cars, and to do it without disabling our own so we could still escape.

At first I thought this might be fun. I imagined a new career in Hollywood as a stunt driver or possibly a secret agent for the IRS. In reality it was far more stressful than I anticipated. The big lesson we learned was that it is not natural for a person to smash into another vehicle on purpose, especially when driving backwards at 30 mph. Despite any claims to the contrary, auditor training was poor preparation for this kind of stunt work.

The "Bang" portion of the course began with an all-day presentation on IEDs (Improvised Explosive Devices). Our instructor, a former Special Forces Officer, shared many of his real life stories and videos while demonstrating the effects of IEDs. His lesson provided the class with excellent advice on how to identify potential suicide bombers and IEDs. At the end, he passed around disarmed IEDs recovered from the streets of Iraq.

As I handled this ordinance I began to get a bad feeling. I imagined how the shrapnel from these bombs, mortars, and rockets would feel as they penetrated my body and realized that this was a very real possibility.

My consolation was that I was no longer stressed by our crash-up derby. I was too busy thinking about getting blown up!

Another all-day training session involved first-aid triage. The medic instructor, who was a former Special Forces soldier, had an excellent sense of humor – a must for anyone helping trauma victims. He taught us how to triage patients after cataclysmic events such as suicide bombings, rocket explosions, and chemical attacks.

One lesson involved a role-playing exercise where I got to play a wounded man. The instructor asked me to lie down and handed me a very realistic fake right arm that lacked a hand. Apparently my hand had been blown off and my fake arm had a bone sticking out of it covered with blood and hanging flesh. The instructor then placed my blown-off right hand into my left hand to hold.

The instructor provided training on how to give first-aid and deal with the psychology of such cases. Apparently this kind of scenario was so common that there was a script for the whole thing:

1. The victim will ask for someone to help him or her take care of the hand.
2. You respond by consoling the victim.
3. Next, put the hand in ice if it's available or wrap the hand in sterile cloth.
4. Finally, ask the victim to hold the hand in his or her good hand. Victims always agree to this because nobody wants to lose their hand.

While I appreciated the brilliant logic and psychology of this advice, the first-aid class was making that bad feeling worse instead of better. I started to have serious doubts about my choice of employment.

Despite these twinges of foreboding, I had to admit that the first-aid instructor was a genuinely fun guy. When we broke for lunch I had the good fortune to sit next to him, and he had all of us in stitches with his jokes and stories from Iraq.

Toward the end of our meal I made the mistake of asking whether he had lost any friends there. The laughing stopped instantly and the instructor stared at me silently for a long time. Finally, in a slow measured voice, he replied, "Yes…Many friends…I have lost many friends over there."

The final day of our "Crash and Bang" course included weapons training. This was the most exciting part of the course because we learned to shoot some serious weaponry. We trained on standard U.S. military issue machine guns, AK-47s, and two kinds of pistol: a Sig Sauer and a Glock. With this course under my belt I knew I was ready for even the most hostile audit anywhere in the world.

As exciting as this training was, it raised a troubling question because there was no plan for me to get a gun. If they weren't issuing me a weapon, then why was I getting weapons training?

No one was willing to answer this question. Finally, after several requests, one of the instructors motioned me aside. In whispered tones he explained that I was getting this training because I might be caught in Baghdad's Red Zone with a security detail that gets ambushed. If a gun were to "fall into my lap" – that is, if the armed guard got killed – I'd at least have a chance to defend myself. All of this was hushed knowledge, though, and never discussed openly. Apparently I was now in a place where certain subjects were off-limits – not a comforting thought, given all of the questions rushing through my head. This company orientation was straying far from the ones I was used to!

With a new appreciation of how dangerous this attractive opportunity to see the Middle East actually was, I called my wife, reminded her how to collect my life insurance, and told her which songs I wanted for my funeral.

While preparing to leave for Iraq, I spent several weeks at the OIG MERO Headquarters in Rosslyn, Virginia, just across the Potomac River from Washington, DC.

On my first day, I walked into the office and found a familiar scene: dozens of cubicles providing workspaces for over 50 auditors. I quickly found my cubicle in the section for new Middle East Auditors and began to organize my desk. However, when I happened to glance over at the next cubicle, I was surprised to see someone old enough to be my Dad. I hadn't expected to see a white-haired senior citizen shipping off to serve in Iraq!

Fortunately this gentleman's disposition was also like my Dad's – quick-witted and kind-hearted, with a wisdom sharpened by occasional bouts of grumpiness. His name was Richard. After a few coffee breaks and lunches together, we discovered that we got along wonderfully.

After my third day at the office, we received a housing form for Baghdad and learned that all living units were to be shared. When Richard reached the part that asked whether he had a preferred flatmate, he asked whether we could select each other because we were both nonsmokers. Considering that I didn't know anyone else and would definitely prefer a non-smoker to a smoker, I replied, "Sure!"

I had no idea how momentous this decision would turn out to be. As two members of a three-member team, and as flatmates, Richard and I saw each other every day, for hours a day, for the next eleven months. This was not because we were particularly fond of each other. It was just the way things were inside the confined boundaries of the Embassy, where we worked together, ate together, and kicked back at the flat together. In addition, we were auditors living among the people we audited, making us slightly more popular than lepers and leaving us with no choice but to form our own colony.

Fortunately Richard was about the best flatmate I could have hoped for. He was quiet, accommodating, and easy to get along with. For example, while other flatmates battled over their showers because there was only enough hot water for one person, we worked out a system where I showered at night and he showered in the morning. Months later, other Embassy residents marveled at our camaraderie after so many days in close quarters. Not only did we work and sleep within twenty feet of each other, we frequently ate together too. In contrast, other flatmates tried to spend as little time together as possible.

During our second week in Rosslyn at OIG headquarters, an African-American auditor named Herb joined our cubicle area. He was a 60-something retired senior FSO (Foreign Service Officer) with a Ph.D., who realized after a few years that there had to be more to his life than just fishing the canals of Ft. Lauderdale.

We soon discovered that Herb was extremely insightful and hilariously funny. He also had a wealth of knowledge on the inner workings and politics of the State Department, as well as unique diplomatic skills that he appeared to have learned by growing up in the segregated south of Gainesville, Florida. The man was unflappable, and managed to keep his sense of humor regardless of the bureaucratic mix-ups or rocket attacks around us.

While Herb had experienced pervasive discrimination in his youth, everything changed when he joined the Air Force, and for this he was deeply grateful. He felt like the Air Force had given him real opportunities and treated him fairly, and he expressed no bitterness over his early days. His career had progressed from enlisted man to senior FSO in the State Department, and he had been able to play a lead-by-example role in our country's transformation into an integrated society.

With the addition of his talents, our team was complete. It was now November and we felt ready for our assignment in Baghdad.

Plunging Into Jordan

November 2008

Because of Herb's experience with Embassy protocol, he flew to Baghdad ahead of Richard and me and prepared the way for our team. As for us relative greenhorns, the trek to Baghdad included a stopover for the weekend in Amman, the capital of Jordan. Our goal was to have an informal orientation on Friday afternoon at the OIG Middle East Regional office, located in Amman's U.S. Embassy. Then, after a restful weekend recovering from jetlag and our orientation, we planned to leave for Baghdad Monday morning.

That was the plan. However, as frequently happens, our flight was delayed, so by the time Richard and I arrived in Jordan the Embassy switchboard had closed for the weekend. Aside from futile messages to our boss' voicemail, there was no way to communicate with him and make plans to meet over the weekend. It was also impossible for us to postpone our departure for Baghdad, so the orientation was off. Resigned to being oriented over a speaker phone after arriving in Baghdad, and with nothing else to do, we gave ourselves a new weekend mission: tour the city and absorb the local culture.

It was dark by the time we left the airport, and as we rode to the hotel I watched the islands of artificial light pass by. These streetlights revealed how parched Jordan's landscape was. A more accurate term would have been "sandscape," because what we saw was a desert devoid of trees, except for the few planted by hand and watered by irrigation. As for the architecture, Amman was like other parts of the developing world I'd seen, except for its abundance of minarets and mosques.

There was something else about Amman that made it different from the other cities I'd visited. The islands of illumination revealed that most of the women wore headscarves. This came as a surprise because my travel book said that Jordan was a secular country.

After registering at the hotel, I waited in the lobby for Richard so that we could go to dinner together. While I was standing there I noticed what looked like a big trick-or-treater in a black sheet float by. This entity was thoroughly concealed and unidentifiable. Only her eyes showed, and even they were barely visible through a narrow slit.

I quickly inferred that I was looking at a woman who was completely covered by what I later learned was an abaya topped with a niqab.[2] Next to her was her bearded and ornery-looking husband.

I resisted the urge to stare, which turned out to be a wise choice. Richard later told me of a time when an old friend had looked too long at a fully-covered woman in an elevator. Her sheik husband responded by yelling and threatening him with his fists.

After Richard arrived we walked to a smoky local restaurant for a cheap meal of roasted chicken and lamb that was shaved from a large pole. Despite the smell of stale smoke, the food was delicious. The restaurant's simple interior consisted of about ten wooden tables and some rickety chairs. In the back was a TV bolted to the wall, blaring a program where an imam chanted the Quran in hypnotic tones. As I listened I wondered, "When was the last time I was in an American restaurant where the TV had someone reciting the Bible?" The answer was, "Never."

The next morning, Richard and I took a taxi to an ancient Roman Theater with an adjacent museum. The driver asked where we were from,

---

2   An abaya is a long over garment essentially a robe-like dress, worn by some women in parts of the Islamic world. A niqab, is a face veil covering all but the eyes. See http://en.wikipedia.org/wiki/Abaya .

and when we replied, "the U.S.," he told us that he was from Ramallah, in Palestine. After starting the car he turned on the radio and played a song with a lot of Allahu Akbars and Muhammads in it. After the song we heard another cleric chant from the Quran. I wondered to myself if the driver ever considered whether or not his American passengers would want to hear these programs.

This experience contrasted with a very different one in China several years earlier. At one point on that trip I had taken a taxi whose driver was playing Buddhist music. As soon as we started to move, he turned off the tape. When I asked him to turn it back on because I enjoyed it, he was surprised. He had conscientiously turned off his religious music because he thought it might not be pleasing to my American ears.

The ruins at the Roman Theater were spectacular, but its Museum was a bit disappointing. For while it had many well-kept displays of Islamic artifacts, protected in climate-controlled cases, the more ancient Byzantine[3] mosaics lay in a dusty common area exposed to human touch and possible damage.

After buying our tickets, we noticed a group of about nine Jordanians standing next to the entrance. As soon as they saw that we had tickets in our hands, they surrounded us in eager competition to be our tour guide. One of them looked particularly wise and grandfatherly, and claimed to speak English, so we hired him. Unfortunately we soon discovered that his knowledge of the language did not exceed his memorized script. He couldn't answer a single question.

He showed us some jewelry containing two fish-like pieces and told us that they represented Jesus feeding five hundred people with two fish. I politely corrected him, saying that Jesus had fed five *thousand* people. He shook his head and replied, "five *hundred* people." I gently but firmly responded, "five *thousand* people." For the next several minutes, as Richard and I inspected the artifacts, we could hear the guide rehearse his updated script to himself: "Five *thousand* people...five *thousand* people...five *thousand* people..."

---

3   The term "Byzantine" is a modern invention identified with the Christian Eastern Roman Empire. While Byzantines themselves would have called themselves Romans, we now call their empire the Byzantine Empire to distinguish it more easily from the Western Roman Empire.

Later in the day we visited The Citadel, an impressive collection of Roman, Byzantine, and Umayyad[4] Islamic ruins, located prominently on the highest hill in Amman. It was a remarkable mash-up of civilizations that included the remains of a Temple to the demigod Hercules from the 2nd century, a Byzantine Church from the 5th century, and a mosque and governor's palace from the Umayyad dynasty in the 8th century. As I looked over these ruins, which were practically on top of each other, I thought about the cataclysmic cultural changes that the people who lived here must have experienced from one generation to the next.

We could also see why the people of these cultures would want to build some of their greatest monuments on this spot: the views were spectacular. In fact, this area was so attractive that its use as a capital went all the way back to the Old Testament Ammonites, after whom the city was named. As we contemplated the view, I realized that we were looking on the very battlefield where Uriah died when King David schemed to take Uriah's wife Bathsheba for himself.[5] No wonder ancient history lived on so vividly here!

Scanning the modern city skyline, I counted sixteen minarets but didn't see a single church steeple. This seemed odd because I had heard that Jordan's population was at least 6% Christian. When I mentioned this to Richard, who had spent nine months in Jordan back in 2004, he told me that the laws for new church construction or even repairs were very restrictive.

Later we visited another museum with fascinating artifacts, including remnants of the Dead Sea Scrolls and an exotic two-foot-tall plaster ancestor statue from about 6500 BC. This statue, along with about thirty others, was discovered in 1983 during road construction on the outskirts of Amman.[6]

As I contemplated these artifacts, I was awestruck by the richness and depth of the culture here. Coming from a country that considers anything

---

4   From the Umayyad dynasty, which was the dynasty of the Islamic Empire that began with the death of Uthman, the 3rd "rightly guided" caliph to lead the Muslims after Muhammad's death in 653 AD, and consolidated it's power over the Islamic Empire following the death of Ali, the 4th "rightly guided" caliph in 661 AD. The first 4 caliphs to lead the Islamic world after Muhammad's death were considered "rightly guided" because they knew Muhammad personally and could therefore claim that they understood the intentions of Muhammad, a claim that none of the later caliphs could make.

5   See 2 Samuel, chapters 11 and 12.

6   For more information, see www.art-and-archaeology.com/jordan/amman/am01.html

more than two hundred years old to be ancient, it was like a fantasy to be surrounded by buildings and artifacts that could be more than two *thousand* years old. With every step, I felt like I was walking on undiscovered history that might suddenly reveal itself if I kicked up the dirt.

As we reflected on these exhibits it dawned on me that the Middle East itself was a kind of living artifact – a bustling open-air time capsule where the past was always present. In fact, people couldn't escape the past here even if they wanted to.

After a day of touring, we returned to the restaurant where we had eaten before. To our amazement the same cleric was still on TV and still chanting from the Quran. As far as we could tell, he was going through it from start to finish!

After dinner we visited a roasted nut shop where Richard purchased a handful of pistachios. I noticed that the scale showed both the weight and the Jordanian dinar amount, which was $JD0.65. However the salesperson charged him $JD2.50. Richard wasn't happy about paying four times the official price, but as a tourist on unfamiliar turf he didn't want an argument, so he paid the inflated amount and we left.

This episode was a shame because I had gotten the impression that, overall, Jordanians were quite hospitable. We resisted the urge to let this experience sour our opinion of the entire country and went back to the hotel to prepare for our trip to Iraq.

The next morning we headed to Marka International Airport, which was located near the Marka Palestinian Refugee Camp, though we never actually saw it. This regional airport was used by our U.S. military for flights between Jordan and Iraq.

In retrospect, Amman resembled a Western city far more than I had appreciated when we first arrived. It was relatively modern and had good shopping, pleasant hotels, and easy access to high-speed Internet. We hadn't really left home yet, or at least that's what I realized once we arrived in Iraq.

"Flight to Baghdad!"

November to December 2008

Our transition from the familiar to the bizarre began at Marka Airport, where we beheld a scene of utter chaos as soon as we entered its doors. There were hundreds of people wandering in front of us, wearing nothing but white bath towels connected by safety pins. Adding confusion to the mix was an acute lack of signage or helpful employees. The combination produced a truly alien scene.

After navigating our way through the turmoil, we discovered that the toweled travelers were Hajj pilgrims on their way to Mecca. We also learned that their outfits, called ihram, were a required part of the pilgrimage. However there was no requirement for the Hajjis to wear these outfits before arriving at the Great Mosque in Mecca. At the airport, the garb was simply a fashion statement.

Among the pilgrims were some American diplomats, looking about as bewildered and out of place as penguins at a beach party. They were also trying to get to Baghdad, so we formed a posse and began to search for our departure gate.

Among these diplomats was a Jewish-American contractor named Carol, who was returning to the Baghdad Embassy from a recent R&R trip to Israel.

As we approached the customs line, we each walked to a different customs agent. Richard and I were cleared within a few minutes, but when we turned to look for Carol, we found that she had disappeared. Assuming that she must have gone to the ladies' room or gotten some food, we continued on.

After clearing customs we had to wait an unspecified but long time for take-off in the terminal's lounge. The reason was security: military flights to Baghdad didn't have published schedules.

The terminal reeked of smoke and stale cigarettes, just like most Jordanian buildings. After waiting long enough for our clothes to absorb the smell of the terminal, an airport official finally called out, "Flight to Baghdad!" We jumped up, grabbed our bags, and rushed outside to breathe some fresh air and catch the shuttle to our plane.

As we boarded the shuttle, we saw a flustered woman racing after us at top speed but hampered by her heavy luggage. Looking closer, we discovered that it was Carol, who managed to jump on-board at the last possible second. In exasperated gasps, she explained that when the Jordanian customs agent noticed the Israeli stamp on her diplomatic passport, he immediately pulled her aside and put her in an isolation room. Agents then interrogated her and made her sit alone for an hour and a half. Finally they let her out at the last minute so that she could still make her flight if she ran non-stop.

She also explained that this form of harassment was, in a sense, her own fault. Travelers with an Israeli stamp on their diplomatic passport were mistreated so systematically in this part of the world that emissaries who traveled to Israel had to keep two passports, even though this wasn't altogether legal. One passport received Israeli stamps, while the other was shown to non-Israeli customs agents. This necessity was especially ridiculous because *diplomatic* passports were supposed to expedite movement through customs regardless of the national stamps on them.

As the shuttle stopped at our destination, I looked ahead and saw a C-17 Globemaster III cargo plane, capable of carrying both hummers and tanks simultaneously. It was an awe-inspiring sight.

The C-17 was even more impressive when we stepped into it. Its interior was a yawning cavern whose sides were lined with fold-down seats for human cargo. We took our places and arrived in Baghdad a short hour later.

On the journey I discovered that travel was *different* on a C-17. For one thing, the flight attendants were well-armed U.S. soldiers. For another, we could forget about beverages and pretzels. I suddenly appreciated how pleasant those cramped commuter flights back in the states actually were.

Travel was particularly different when it came to landing at Baghdad International Airport. To avoid surface-to-air-missile attacks, our craft landed using the corkscrew maneuver – a rapid spiral drop that ended with a thud on the tarmac. It was the tallest and best rollercoaster ride I ever had.

Disembarking from the C-17 was also a dramatic experience. As the massive cargo door gaped open to release us, sunlight flooded overhead and a refreshing breeze greeted us with Iraq's 70-degree weather. The clear blue sky promised a picture-perfect day.

Then we walked off the embarking ramp and discovered that we were surrounded by sandbags and twelve-foot tall T-walls that resembled Jersey barriers[7] on steroids. Yellowish-grayish dust covered everything, including the hoard of U.S. soldiers who wielded their machine guns as they hovered around us.

A bulldozer abruptly interrupted our reverie by pulling up and dumping our luggage onto a pallet. I picked up what were now my battered and dusty suitcases and dragged them a hundred yards to the processing building for arrivals. There were no moving sidewalks, of course, so we pulled our luggage across a trail of rough gravel. The drag from the gravel made my suitcases feel like quarter-ton weights.

A short time later we received our 40lb PPE (Personal Protective Equipment), which included a bulletproof vest and combat helmet. My helmet was too big, but there was no time to exchange it because we were quickly told to move on. With my helmet sliding around my head, we hauled our luggage another hundred yards along the same rough gravel to another runway and waited for the helicopters that would take us to the Embassy.

After standing by the runway for an hour, we heard rotors thumping in the distance and looked up to see two large Chinook helicopters coming our way. This was about to be my first ride in a helo – another fantasy made real by this job. My fatigue disappeared as the Chinook's noise and gusts thrilled me like a kid. A few minutes later we and our suitcases were airborne.

---

7   Concrete traffic barriers, often used in the U.S. to separate opposing lanes of traffic from each other.

As we passed over a suburb of Baghdad I saw one of the soldiers pull down a large overhead .50 caliber machine gun and point it at the houses below. I surmised that this wasn't one of the friendlier neighborhoods in town.

From our vantage point Baghdad was surprisingly lush, with its many date palm plantations and fields of grass. The houses below were typical for the Middle East, with flat roofs and open courtyards or patios.

Ahead of us was an empty field where we could see children playing soccer. Just past the children lay an array of bombed-out buildings – lifeless shells of broken concrete that jutted out of the greenery.

A short time later our helo landed at the Washington Heliport of the International Zone (IZ), popularly known as the Green Zone.[8] We took a five-minute shuttle ride to the NEC (New Embassy Compound) and checked into our living quarters as night settled in.

At that time there were two Embassy compounds. The original one was Saddam Hussein's former Republican Palace, due to close on December 31st. The second was the $700 million NEC, which would officially take over as the new Embassy on January 1. Plans were already underway to transfer Embassy offices from the Palace to the NEC, but the new site was still under construction and raising clouds of dust. Many of the cubicles were unfinished, and new office furniture was strewn along the walls in the Chancery,[9] making our offices unusable. With nowhere else to go, our audit team staked out a make-shift workplace in a large building called Annex 1, where we set ourselves up on the third floor in a clean but minimalist suite of cubicles.

Three weeks later, we moved into our new offices in the Chancery. As we inspected our attractive new suite, a half-joking debate arose among the three of us over who'd get the window office. Nobody wanted it! The view was a miserable reminder of our hot and dusty surroundings, and even if it had been nice, nothing could compensate for being the closest man to a potential rocket or suicide bomb attack. Herb, being the true diplomat he

---

8   The International Zone was a four square mile protected area in central Baghdad north of the Tigris River that housed the U.S. and numerous other foreign embassies, along with the U.S. Military, contractor companies and non-governmental organizations. See http://en.wikipedia.org/wiki/Green_Zone.

9   A Chancery is the type of building that houses a diplomatic mission or embassy. An embassy may have multiple buildings, but the Chancery is normally where the ambassador and high level diplomat offices are located.

was, volunteered for "the honor" while Richard and I timidly retreated to our new interior offices.

With our territory staked out, our performance audit team was officially open for business. Of course, our troika couldn't fill out the whole suite of six offices ourselves, so three staff people with SIGIR (Special Inspector General for Iraq Reconstruction) took the rest of the suite.

While this was an innocent and practical arrangement, it also created a mix-up throughout the Embassy that would hang around our necks like an albatross. To understand why, a little background is in order:

SIGIR was a special temporary OIG commissioned by Congress specifically for Iraq. Because of the Embassy's combination of diplomatic and military functions, SIGIR was an audit agency for both the State Department and the Department of Defense (DOD), with jurisdiction throughout the country. SIGIR audits had the potential to damage FSO careers, and its investigators were armed law enforcement officers who could *end* those careers.

Meanwhile, my team's OIG only focused on Embassy programs, where we audited the organization design, staffing, and process effectiveness of various departments. We were performance auditors, and we analyzed systems to reduce waste and inefficiency, often finding ways to save taxpayers thousands or millions of dollars while also creating safer workplaces. While we may have been annoying at times, we rarely endangered anyone's career.

Given that SIGIR had dozens of auditors and investigators throughout the Embassy, they were much more prominent than our low-profile three-man team. Therefore the three who shared office space with us created an opportunity for confusion, and all of the fear and loathing of SIGIR's auditors transferred to us.

One of my team's early experiences with our new pariah status took place during our morning coffees together by the Annex 1 snack room. The snack room was on the first floor and had tables in an adjacent open area that faced a set of elevators. It was a convenient place for us to get together and make our plans for the day, but it had a downside: nearly every FSO who entered the building walked by us on their way to the elevators. On their way, many of them would make remarks about auditors slouching on the job, like "Hey, look at those auditors over there. Don't you have anything better to do than sit around drinking coffee?"

While we took the ribbing good naturedly the first few times, it got annoying after several days. Herb, ever resourceful, finally decided that it was time for *us* to have some fun with *them*. The next time someone made a remark about us sitting there drinking coffee, he replied, "Actually, we're sitting here in order to OBSERVE you."

It only took two times for Herb's comeback to have the desired effect. After that, not a single FSO said a word about our morning coffees.

As for living space, the NEC living quarters consisted of 600 one-bedroom apartments known as SDAs (Single Diplomat Accommodations). Or at least that was the original plan.

It turned out that the staffing surge was so great that the one-bedroom units were magically converted into two-bedroom units. That is, each living room became a bedroom and received a new wall, door, mini-closet, and bed. This left the tiny dining room and kitchen as the only communal living spaces. I imagined how comfortable these residences were originally designed to be.

In our apartment, Richard got the bedroom while I got the former living room, which was slightly larger but had less closet space. The dining area was just big enough to accommodate a square table, and the wooden chairs that came with it were about the flimsiest I'd ever seen. As the months wore on, remnants of these chairs accumulated outside people's rooms and by the dumpster.

There was also a small kitchen with all-new appliances and accoutrements, including a dishwasher, refrigerator, microwave, stove, and cabinets stocked with glasses, plates, mixing bowls, and utensils. I knew the microwave worked because Richard occasionally warmed a frozen pizza in it. Neither of us ever found out whether the oven worked. Looked nice, though.

After showering off the dust that had penetrated our clothes and every crevice, we visited Herb, who had already set up his flat. He warned us about the lackluster quality of food at the NEC's temporary DFAC (Dining Facility), located at the Recreation Building's American Club, and invited us to join him for a shuttle-bus trip to the much larger one at the Republican Palace. We accepted Herb's invitation and enjoyed a delicious dinner of steak and crab legs. These DFAC meals were free to all Embassy Residents – a very savory perk.

As we approached the DFAC entrance we saw a large sand-filled bucket with a big sign sticking out of it. It commanded "Clear your weapons before entering DFAC." Stepping inside, we beheld a sprawling and heavily armed multi-ethnic mass of humanity. There were hundreds of civilians and soldiers eating together, and the latter were carrying pistols and machine guns at their sides or storing them under their chairs.

When people talk about culture shock back in the U.S., they don't have a clue. THIS was culture shock. I had never seen so many guns in my life, and yet they received about as much attention as a spoon.

The next morning I awoke to a beautiful sunny day in an utterly barren environment. The NEC's nickname was "the prison," and it didn't take long to see why. Armed Peruvian security guards paced along its guard towers and we were surrounded by T-walls, razor wire, and a complete lack of landscaping. The subliminal message was, "Your name is now inmate #3421."

When I stepped outside I nearly choked on the acrid smell of burning plastic and garbage. Later I learned that Iraqis burned most of their refuse in open burn pits. Depending on the wind direction, the nearby pits could spew their smoke and black ash all over the Embassy grounds.

Across the Tigris River I saw a large refinery with three smokestacks in the distance, filling the sky with black smoke. This was how the antiquated refinery burned off natural gas. I gathered that environmentalism was not a high priority in this part of the world.

It shouldn't be a surprise that I almost immediately developed a dry hacking cough. In the daytime it hadn't been so bad, but it was brutal at night when I was trying to sleep. I felt a constant irritating tickle that could wake me up and send me into such a coughing spasm that I would gag, unable to breathe. Thinking that I might have gotten some kind of strange disease, I mentioned my cough to Richard and Herb. They responded in concert: "Oh yeah, you have the Baghdad cough. It will clear up in about a month." While they weren't terribly sympathetic, it was a relief to know that my cough was "normal."

That afternoon we returned to the Republican Palace for a tour. It was a majestic sight in daylight, with its beautiful turquoise dome, graceful arches, and porticos beautifully accented by shimmering pools.

The inside was also impressive, with its ten-foot-high hardwood doors and ornate chandeliers hanging in suspended elegance. In Saddam Hussein's

Decision Room, the domed ceiling was festooned with paintings that portrayed Iraqi missiles shooting toward Jerusalem.

The palace got its nickname, "Saddam's Palace," from the ornate tiles covering the walls, all inscribed with Saddam's Arabic initials. I mused upon the kind of person who'd surround himself with his own name.

Repurposed into office space, the Palace's vast interior had lost some of its grandeur because it was now sectioned into cubicles by temporary walls. Despite its diminished luster, it was still far more welcoming than the dusty NEC that my colleagues and I returned to afterwards.

On waking the next morning in my new NEC home, I opened the blinds and discovered that our cramped apartment was actually a beautiful water-view condo! If I twisted my neck in just the right way as I looked out the window, I could see the Tigris River and its adjoining lagoon. Part of me longed to break out a kayak but the thought of having to dodge mortars while paddling dispelled *that* idea fast.

While the NEC's permanent DFAC was under construction, there were times when schedule constraints gave us little choice but to use the temporary DFAC that Herb warned us about. This stop-gap chow hall wasn't exactly Mom's cooking, so we and the other residents ate there as rarely as possible, taking the mile-long shuttle ride to the Palace DFAC whenever we could. This shuttle was a miniature bus with curtains over the side and back windows to make it more difficult for potential attackers to hit their targets.

The Embassy also had a commissary store about the size of a 7 Eleven. Inside it was a selection of clothing, OTC medicines, candy, gum, frozen food, and liquor. When I went to purchase some beer so that Richard and I could celebrate our new apartment together, I discovered that most of the shelves were empty. When I mentioned this to the cashier, he said that a full shipment of alcohol had been delivered yesterday but had already nearly sold out. Apparently drinking was a preferred therapy for the Embassy's desolation and boredom. My own therapy was cough syrup, which I drank like soda to keep my raspy throat under control.

Across from the Embassy were apartment towers where local Iraqis lived. Next to these towers was a new mosque complex, spiked with tall minarets that bristled with loud-speakers. These speakers blared the call-to-prayer so loudly that it penetrated every corner of the Embassy. I could tell that I had a lot of adjusting to do to get used to these new sights, sounds, and air.

Thursday was Thanksgiving Day, so my colleagues and I decided to have dinner together to celebrate. In the company of these good people I made the most of our celebration. All the same, my heart ached to be back home with my wife. Taking in all of the new sights, sounds, smells, people, and procedures was just too much, too fast. That night, after wishing my wife good night and hanging up the phone, I lay awake in bed and wondered, "What am I doing here?"

A week after Thanksgiving, while dining at the Palace DFAC, I happened to meet Colonel Kim, a petite Korean-American with a commanding presence. As we talked, I discovered that she oversaw programs that dealt with Iraqi women's issues and orphans.

My ears pricked up as soon as I heard this because I had been hoping to do some kind of work with local Iraqis. Perhaps there was some way I could assist with one of her programs.

I was particularly interested in the Iraqi orphans because Ping and I had no children and we were open to the possibility of adoption. However the Colonel quickly dispelled this idea when she explained that, according to Islamic law, non-Muslim families could not adopt children born to Muslim parents. The only way Ping and I could adopt one of these adorable children would be for us to convert to Islam. This roadblock was unwelcome news because it meant that my tour in Iraq would postpone our adoption efforts for another year.

During our dinner conversation we were joined by an Army officer who also worked on women's issues. He shared with us a personal story about an Iraqi-made DVD he encountered, which was a training guide on healthy home-life and the proper relations between husband and wife.

Apparently, the Army had been distributing this DVD for a while, so when he got involved with women's issues he decided to take a look at it. As he watched he noticed a scene where the husband slapped his wife over some perceived offense. When he reported that this video promoted domestic violence, the American program leaders were shocked and immediately pulled it from distribution. However the Iraqi leaders in the women's program protested, claiming that such behavior was a part of their culture and that the DVD's distribution should resume.

By December my body was adjusting to life in Baghdad, but my lonely spirit was having a more difficult time. The cough had disappeared, as promised, but twinges of homesickness were threatening to bloom into full-blown cabin fever. This wasn't good because I had been at the Embassy for only a few weeks and still had more than ten months to go.

To shake off my blues, I decided to explore some yet-unknown regions of the NEC. This excursion brought me to the indoor swimming pool at the semi-completed Recreation Building, which became one of my daily diversions. Still, the options for exercise and fun were sparse.

One of these options was the outdoor swimming pool and garden at the Republican Palace, which was only a short shuttle ride away. Despite its limited value as an alternative to the indoor swimming pool, it was an oasis of calm in a chaotic environment. With its soothing palms and chirping birds, it felt more like a Florida vacation than Iraq. Of course, shuttling back from these vacations to the NEC prompted a miniature replay of the culture shock I felt on first arrival.

Among the cultural issues for me to adjust to were the Iraqi customs for conflict resolution. In Western culture we usually pursue disagreements through written or verbal dialogue. In Iraq, common methods included screaming matches, guns, mortars and/or rockets.

At 6:15 one morning I was shocked awake by the alarm of an emergency system called "The Big Voice." The alarm blasted an alternating high-low sound and then bellowed:

"DUCK AND COVER! GET AWAY FROM THE WINDOWS! TAKE COVER AND WAIT FOR FURTHER INSTRUCTIONS!"

From our training we knew that incoming rockets were about to land. After such an announcement we had less than ten seconds to throw on our PPE and find a secure location. In this environment we learned to wake up FAST. No snooze buttons!

While hiding behind the couch I awaited and finally heard the intercom announce what later became a familiar refrain:

"This is the command post. ALL CLEAR, I SAY ALL CLEAR."

This announcement meant there were no other imminent rocket attacks and we could go back to what we were doing.

Later I learned that a rocket had landed near the UN Headquarters, just a mile away. It killed two and injured fifteen.[10] All the dead and injured were South-Asian catering workers who supported the UN Staff. These victims were people who, like me, had traveled far from home to earn money for their families. What Iraq sent back was something very different.

Several days after the rocket attack I felt a different kind of explosion. This time it was in my head, caused by a steep pressure drop from a fast-rising storm. The rushing wind kicked up a gritty smog of sand and dust and, within minutes, ominous clouds burst with thunder and lightning in a rare torrential downpour that flooded the Republican Palace's basement.

Winter was Iraq's rainy season, but this flood was apparently one for the record books. It even managed to drown Baghdad's drainage system, making the culverts spew water rather than drain it. The whole place was miserable, muddy, and wet.

10 *Rocket kills two in Green Zone*, by Tina Susman, *Los Angles Times,* November, 30, 2008. See http://articles.latimes.com/2008/nov/30/world/fg-iraq30 .

Christmas Vacation

December to January 2008

The wet grimy days of Baghdad's rainy season slowly ticked away until it was finally December 20th – time for my escape home for Christmas. Thanks to some astute negotiating at the beginning of my engagement, I had received a three-week consultation trip back to DC so I could be with family while continuing to work over the holiday. However, despite my family's legitimate needs, I felt guilty for leaving my colleagues in Baghdad's winter wonderland of mud.

The procedure for heading home started with a NEC shuttle bus to the Washington Heliport, located across the street from the Presidential Palace. After arriving at the pad, we waited in a dusty helo-hanger for the seven-minute flight to Baghdad International Airport. Our plan was to spend the night next to the airport in the Sully Compound "Inn," a complex of plumbing-free dry trailers that were furnished with two beds each. On the back of each trailer's door was a sign notifying residents that "anyone who urinates into empty water bottles while a guest will permanently lose Sully privileges." Our less convenient alternative was a latrine several minutes away. I later got to know the muddy trail that led to it when I got up to use it at 2 AM, when it was 30-odd degrees outside.

On arriving we discovered that so many people were going home for Christmas that there was literally no room at the Inn. Therefore we spent the night in a nearby makeshift tent with a couple dozen new-found friends.

Few of us got much sleep that night. In addition to the constant human motion and a symphony of snores, the tent shook loudly every few minutes from the vibrations of low flying planes and helicopters. We finally arose with the cold gray rays of the dust-clouded sun, feeling about as cold and gray as the morning itself.

Following breakfast at the Victory Base DFAC located next to the airport, we continued to the military terminal and waited for our C-17 to Amman.

On landing in Amman I suddenly had a new appreciation for the place. It felt like Disneyland, complete with stores, gas stations, and even fast-food restaurants!

What I noticed most was what I *didn't* see: the guards, concrete T-walls, and razor wire that had surrounded me for the past month. I had escaped "the prison."

From Amman I took a connecting flight with a four-hour layover in London's Heathrow Airport. Finally, three days after my journey had started, I was holding my beautiful Ping at the airport in Washington, DC. I felt overwhelmed, as relief and a flood of pent-up emotion rushed over me. Then I thought about what it was like for a combat-hardened soldier to come home to people who could no longer understand him, and also the Americans who had to stay in Iraq over the holidays. I was one of the lucky ones.

The next day we drove from our home in northern Virginia to Batavia, a small town in Western New York, to see my parents and other relatives for Christmas. On the way, I began to realize how much that month in Iraq had changed me.

It felt strange to not stop at a single military checkpoint during the entire eight-hour trip. I was also intensely aware of every bridge, cliff, and blind corner. As we approached each structure I scanned it instinctively for potential attackers.

On Christmas Eve we went to the service at my parent's church. I almost panicked at its lack of security, with its entrances completely unguarded and not even locked. It was an open invitation for a suicide bomber to walk right in!

Then I realized that my fears were ridiculous. With a sigh of relief I realized how *good* it was to be home again. I began to appreciate my family, my wife, the snow, the trees, and the quiet freedom of just being able to walk outside as never before. I also recognized how much we took for granted in the United States. Most people are incapable of even *imagining* how different their lives could be.

The days disappeared all too quickly, and before I knew it it was January 10th – time to return to Baghdad. Ping accompanied me to Dulles International Airport and we shared our last kisses goodbye. Then I exiled myself back into the sky.

Our flight was delayed for four-hours in London, so I used the intermission to page through an English-language Quran that I had recently purchased. After hearing the Quran so frequently in stores and cabs around Jordan and listening to the five prayer-calls each day at the NEC, I felt that I didn't have much choice but to buy one. It had become clear that the Quran was woven deeply into the fabric of life in the Middle East, and if I ever wanted to understand Iraq I had better understand that book.

As I awaited my flight I flipped through the Quran and noticed a verse in surah[11] 3:28:[12]

> *Let not the believers {Muslims} take for friends or helpers unbelievers rather than believers: if any do that, in nothing will there be help from Allah.*

I wondered, "What does *that* mean? – that I'll never have a genuine Muslim friend?"

Because of the long delay in London I didn't arrive at the Grand Hyatt in Amman until 3:00 AM. However I still had to get up by 7:00 AM for the ride to Marka Airport and my flight to Baghdad.

After another hour-long flight, I hopped out of the C-17 with the other passengers and took in a blast of cold clammy air. Clouds had rolled into Baghdad and a light misty rain was falling. Everywhere I looked there was either mud or muddy brown water. Nothing had changed since I had left.

---

11   The chapters of the Quran are called surahs.
12   *The Holy Qur-an: Text, Translation, and Commentary*, by Yusuf Ali, 1934.

Soon we were dragging our suitcases along the coarse gravel-and-mud trail toward the helipad again for our flight to the NEC. Thirty-six hours after leaving DC, I was back in "the prison" and exhausted.

As I lumbered back to my SDA, I noticed that my impression of the Embassy felt different this time. There was no culture shock. I realized that the NEC was becoming a part of me and I a part of it. That night, as visions of Christmas danced in my head, I slept like a baby in my government-issued bed.

A Tour of the Green Zone

January 2009

On Saturday, January 17th, I leapt out of bed and put on my best casual clothes. This was going to be a special day because I had read an advertisement saying that a group of Embassy residents had organized an interdenominational chapel service. I was about to worship at an Embassy chapel for the first time.

One of the first questions that occurred to me when I saw this opportunity was, "Why Saturday?" I subsequently found out, after getting to know one of the service's prime organizers – a dynamic evangelist named Robin Rowan. Organizing this worship service had been no easy task, and Saturday was as close to Sunday as they could get.

Originally, when the U.S. Embassy was at the Republican Palace, worship services were held in an adjacent hooch (more formally known as a Containerized Housing Unit, or CHU). This chapel served a variety of denominations throughout the day and evening each Sunday, along with a Saturday night Mass for Catholics. These services were all officiated by Army Chaplains and served both the Embassy and the military personnel stationed nearby.

However, a problem arose when the Embassy moved to the NEC: someone decided that the Embassy was to conform with the workweek of Iraq, as U.S. Embassies often do in relation to their host countries.

In Iraq, as in most other Islamic countries, the work week went from Sunday through Thursday, with Friday being Islam's holy day. This made Sunday worship nearly impossible for the Embassy's predominantly Christian population because everyone was expected to be at work.

To make matters worse, the Embassy's chapel was transferred to Camp Union, located across the street from the Embassy. This was a problem because Embassy employees couldn't leave the Embassy on their own. SNAFU or otherwise, the Embassy's logisticians were on the verge of snuffing out Christian worship at the Embassy.

The Embassy's Christian employees were distraught when they suddenly found themselves on Iraqi soil without even the comfort of their worship services. Upon discovering this fiasco, Robin became a pit bull at the heels of the Army Chaplains. She begged and pleaded relentlessly for a Saturday morning service at the NEC.

Finally, Chaplain Katz, the leader of the contemporary service, agreed to conduct the services if an on-Embassy location could be found. Robin immediately reserved a conference room in Annex 1 and, with the help of Dan, her guitar-playing friend and worship leader, they rounded up a small choir and held their first service, for a congregation of seven. Her next move was to advertise the worship service through the Community Events department of the Embassy, and that's how I found out about it.

The number of attendees had already grown considerably since the first service a week earlier. Joining me were seven women, twenty-one men, and five guns. This service had the unique distinction of being the first one I had ever attended where parishioners openly packed heat.

Everything about this service was beautiful, and the familiar music and kind faces transported me to a homier place, if only for a little while. I sensed that the NEC was slowly becoming more humane and losing the prison-like atmosphere I had first encountered. Without realizing who was responsible, I was thankful for all of the effort that Robin, Dan, and Chaplain Katz had gone through.

After the service, I left for my next appointment: A tour of the Green Zone.

There were two practical requirements for sightseeing in the Green Zone: a car and a gun. Because I had neither, I had been feeling locked down at the NEC. Thankfully my friend Tony, a long-term resident and SIGIR investigator from our office, had both, and arranged to show me around the grounds.

Our first stop was the July 14 Bridge,[13] home of a checkpoint that went into the Red Zone. We pulled into a grungy parking lot and stepped out among the crushed plastic bottles and cigarette butts to look around.

On our left was a short line of cars waiting to clear the checkpoint and enter the Red Zone. I asked Tony why soldiers were inspecting these vehicles. After all, they were leaving the Green Zone, not entering it. He replied that they did this to prevent people from kidnapping Americans or smuggling out weapons or secrets.

Careful to avoid the cars in case one blew up, we walked over to the pedestrian side of the bridge. I peered over the murky oil-slicked waters of the Tigris and inhaled the foul air. The scene wasn't pretty, but it *was* memorable.

Our next stop was the turquoise-colored lagoon that Saddam had made for his sons Uday and Qusay. It looked like a lake-sized gravel-lined swimming pool, complete with a filtration system that kept it crystal clear. This had been the private recreation pond where Uday and Qusay water skied with their guests. After the war the U.S. repaired the filtration system and restored the lagoon's brilliant clarity, drawing a sharp contrast to the neighboring Tigris's oily brown.

We then drove along the causeway that separated the Tigris from the brothers' lagoon and stopped near some ramshackle park benches to look around. We had to walk carefully, though, to avoid the trash that completely covered the shorelines and spilled into the water on both sides. Broken beer bottles, plastic bags, and old shoes lay among the refuse, making the park look like the local dump.

Our third stop brought us to Camp Liberty, which in many ways resembled a Northern Virginia swim-club. Among its sundry diversions were a large outdoor swimming pool, beach chairs, and barbecue grills.

---

13 Named after the July 14, 1958 revolution, which overthrew the Iraqi monarchy and established the Iraqi Republic.

As we parked across the street Tony told me a story about Camp Liberty. A few months earlier, in that very parking lot, he and a co-worker had returned to their SUV and found two Iraqis' leaning over each side of its front bumper. Thinking that the men were planting a bomb, Tony and his partner pulled their guns, positioned themselves on either side, and yelled "Freeze!" It was at this point they discovered that their terror suspects had been urinating. All the Iraqis managed to plant were some puddles.

Our next objective was to pay our respects at the Tomb of the Unknown Soldier in Zawra Park, which at the time was part of the Green Zone. This monument was built in the wake of the Iran-Iraq War (1980-88), which began when Saddam Hussein, a Sunni, invaded Shiite-controlled Iran to take advantage of the internal turmoil caused by Iran's 1979 revolution. Although the war produced no territorial gains for Iraq, it managed to kill a half a million Iranians in exchange for only 200,000 Iraqis. As we walked around its festival and parade grounds, the memorials gave the impression that Saddam's "victory" was the excessive number of Iranians killed, given that little else was accomplished.

The festival and parade ground, which was the size of several football fields, was bookended by a famous pair of Crossed Swords arches. A wide avenue led from each arch to the center of the complex where the Tomb of the Unknown Soldier lay.

Before visiting the tomb we stopped at one of the Crossed Swords and took some photos. These arches were filled with bloody symbolism: The swords themselves were made from melted-down weapons recovered from dead Iraqi soldiers, while the arms holding the swords were modeled after Saddam Hussein's own. Finally, at the base of each arm, there were strewn the helmets of thousands of dead Iranians in order to celebrate their deaths.

After photographing the arches, we moved on to the majestic Tomb of the Unknown Soldier – a giant shield that floated over the coffin of an actual unknown Iraqi. The tomb also had an underground museum, but it was closed to the public at the time.

Iraqi guards carrying AK-47s protected the entrance to the grounds, so Tony asked whether it was okay for us to go in. One of the guards responded by talking in Arabic on his two-way radio for several minutes, apparently seeking permission. Finally he turned to us and said that we could, on the condition that we emptied our weapons.

Because the guard spoke no English and I spoke only a few words of Arabic, I lifted my jacket to show that I wasn't carrying a weapon. This satisfied him and soon one of the guards was escorting us around the complex, wearing a big smile the whole time. He was a non-stop talker, but he had the courtesy to speak very slowly and clearly. What he failed to realize was that, no matter how slowly he spoke, we were not going to understand him because we didn't speak Arabic. I wished that I had paid more attention to my language tapes a few nights before and resolved to do better. However, despite the language barrier, the soldiers' visible pride told of the reverence and honor this monument gave to the terrible losses Iraq suffered from Saddam Hussein's adventurism.

The Tomb, located on a small hill, rose at least five-stories and offered a scenic bird's eye view of Baghdad. I was impressed by its noble and majestic lines. In fact, Baghdad was filled with impressive monuments, many of which were still standing.

After taking a panorama of photos, it was time for lunch at Camp Prosperity, another one of the U.S. Military Bases. Camp Prosperity stood within the Al-Salam Palace compound, a palace with a truly Saddamesque story behind it:

In 1995 Saddam's two daughters and sons-in-law had defected to Jordan, where the men had bad-mouthed Saddam's regime and disclosed blood-stained secrets. Saddam responded by luring them back to Iraq with an offer to build the Al-Salam Palace for them. He claimed that he missed them and would forgive them if only they'd return. Once they arrived, though, Saddam's proxies nabbed the sons-in-law and killed them.

This palace was a victim of the 2003 "shock and awe" campaign and it remained unrepaired. However, Camp Prosperity arose from the ruins and the palace gardens now showcased shops and restaurants. At one of these restaurants I enjoyed my first authentic Iraqi meal since arriving in the country – a delicious combination of ground lamb, chicken, hummus, and bread. Lunch marked the end of our tour and we rode back to the NEC.

The Mission

January to March 2009

One of our audit objectives was to examine the operating effectiveness of the Regional Embassy Offices. On January 20th we rose early, ate breakfast, donned our PPE, and headed to the NEC shuttle-bus stop to begin the project.

In this case our "bus" was an armored SUV that ferried us to the Embassy's helipad. Our plan was to take a tour of the REO (Regional Embassy Office) near King Nebuchadnezzar's[14] hometown of Babylon (Al-Hillah), about 60 miles south of Baghdad.

Richard, Herb, and I squeezed into a tiny "bluebird" helicopter with the other passengers for the 45-minute ride. To get a sense of how tightly we were squeezed, imagine a closed zipper. The passengers were seated on opposite sides of the bluebird, which was so narrow that each passenger's knees went into the crotches of the two passengers opposite him or her, so that our legs looked like the teeth of a zipper. As we flew along we had a keen awareness that it would only take one hard landing for us to be singing soprano for the rest of our lives.

---

14 Nebuchadnezzar II, king of the Neo-Babylonian Empire from 605 BC to 562 BC. He is mentioned in the Bible in Jeremiah 4:7, Jeremiah 52, and Daniel 3 & 4.

We flew very low, and at times were skimming just above the treetops. We did this for security reasons because it was more difficult for enemy ground fire to target us while flying at such low altitudes.

After passing over the usual bombed-out buildings and garbage piles of the city we found ourselves flying over that green and beautiful Iraq we had only glimpsed in my previous helo rides. This belt of lush fertility followed the Tigris and provided endless miles of verdant farmland, irrigation channels, and date-palm plantations.

Sometimes we flew so low that we felt like we were about to drop in on one of the open-air living rooms of the mud-colored homes below. We'd look down to see people sipping tea in their yards or herding their cows and goats. Often they'd look up and smile or wave to us, as if inviting us to stop in. While I expected to see children get excited about a helicopter, it was fun to see adults do it too.

All of the women I saw in the countryside wore traditional black abayas, leaving them virtually indistinguishable from each other. I could only imagine how uncomfortable they would feel in the 120+ degree summer heat.

Our mission included quick landings at a pair of FOBs (Forward Operating Bases) in the desert, far removed from the beautiful scenery we had recently overflown. Each FOB was an island of T-Walls that bristled with barbed wire, which surrounded a complex of big guns, sand bags, and drab concrete structures. From ground level the FOBs looked out on a desolate treeless landscape as far as the eye could see. The Embassy I griped about was a luxury resort compared to what the soldiers in those FOBs endured.

Forty-five minutes into the flight, a fellow passenger pointed out Babylon and another one of Saddam's giant palaces, sitting on a giant man-made hill. A short time later we approached the city of Al-Hillah and its famous Babylon Hotel.

When the hotel appeared on the horizon it looked like a remodeled crusader castle. It dwarfed the nearby buildings and had an expansive system of T-walls made necessary by its new tenant, the REO. As impressive as it looked, and despite its role in American diplomacy, we learned that these features were not the hotel's claim to fame. Apparently the Babylon Hotel had long been famous as *the* "temporary marriage honeymoon hotel," thanks to the Shiite religious foundation that owned it. This visit was about to be my introduction to the Shiite institution of temporary marriage.

One of the Senior Foreign Service Officers stationed in Al-Hillah explained to us that in Shiite (but not Sunni) Islam, men may contract temporary wives for specified periods of time. These periods could range from an hour, to six months, to ten years or more. At the end of the contract, the marriage ends and the temporary husband pays his temporary bride the agreed-upon price. This payment may be anything from clothing to jewelry, livestock, or money. Also, the contractor of a temporary marriage must be the bride's father or another male relative designated as her guardian.

This arrangement may sound similar to what goes on in Nevada. However, it has the unique distinction of using a close male relative to act as the woman's "guardian."

Later I learned that while temporary marriage is a normal practice among the Shiites of Iraq, Sunnis call it either fornication – a crime punishable by 80 whiplashes – or adultery – a crime punishable by death. This conflict in religious law provided me with a sharp insight into why animosities between Sunnis and Shiites were so fierce and intractable. It also made me wonder about the dilemmas such religiously-approved practices could create if large numbers of Shiites migrated to the United States. Would we have to respect this form of prostitution as an expression of religious freedom?

While I presumed that our leaders chose the Babylon Hotel as a REO site because of its size instead of its claim to fame, the hotel's dual purpose provided another valuable insight: it revealed the kinds of compromises we made to operate in this part of the world.

After a day of meetings and a tour of the 24-acre REO compound, I relaxed and watched the sun glide down toward the horizon. That is, we stood and waited nearly two hours at the helipad for our flight.

Finally we heard the welcome roar of blue birds in the distance and gave a collective sigh of relief. This was because, during our wait, some of the folks told us of times when they had been stuck at this REO for days with nothing to do but contemplate the camel spiders.

Little did I know that this round-trip to the REO would be a major highlight of my stay in Iraq. What made it so memorable was its bird's eye tour of the country – a refreshing change from the dusty buildings of the Green Zone that I had come to know all too well.

Back at the Embassy the quality of life continued to slowly improve. Less than a year earlier, people like me were experiencing daily rocket attacks at the old Republican Palace. For example, there was a time when my boss in Jordan, who had previously worked in Baghdad, held an outdoor meeting by the Republican Palace pool with his staff. This was a common practice because the Embassy staff had outgrown the palace and the conference rooms were frequently booked. A rocket partially exploded in a tree over his group and gouged him with shrapnel, leaving him half-deaf in one ear. If the rocket had exploded completely, I would have had a different boss.

Far worse were the rocket barrages that began on Easter Sunday of 2008, just a few months before I arrived. At that time the Green Zone had endured more than three weeks of steady attacks. Over an eight-day period in late March, terrorists launched more than a hundred rockets into the Zone.

These rockets struck the Embassy in the Republican Palace, the U.S. helicopter pad, the vehicle fleet, and several hooches. Tragically, they killed five people, including Paul Converse (a fellow auditor from SIGIR), and wounded 39 others. It was the most damaging rocket bombardment in the history of the Embassy. In its wake, embassy staff were prohibited by security from leaving the building and had to sleep on cots in their respective offices for several days.

Fortunately the Embassy's security situation had improved by the time I arrived. We still had duck-and-cover alarms, but Iraqi-on-Iraqi bombings were far more common than attacks directed at us.

On several occasions I heard car-bomb explosions or AK-47 gunfights during my walks to the DFAC. This gave me something to reflect on while I ate, namely the innocent people who had just lost their lives for no sane reason. From this I inferred that the security "improvement" meant that, instead of dodging attacks myself, I got to witness Iraqis dodging attacks.

As much as our situation had improved prior to my arrival, the memories of those dire days were still fresh, and I constantly got into conversations with people sporting battle scars, also known as "Baghdad tattoos".

One of these seasoned veterans was a tough but bubbly Texan named Janet, who served as the Embassy Contracting Officer. She had been one of those wounded during the Easter 2008 attack, and one day she told me about her experience. She had been in the Republican Palace when a rocket landed outside a nearby window. Instantly she had been peppered with glass shards and shrapnel. She told me that she was one of the lucky ones because her wounds healed quickly, though her arm still sported an impressive Baghdad tattoo. Others were not so fortunate, such as the KBR pool attendant who was killed when a rocket landed directly on top of her as she stood next to the pool.

While these stories occasionally made the news back home, what never got mentioned was the collateral damage and terror these random attacks caused. On a fairly regular basis, I would see Embassy residents hobbling on crutches, only to find out that they had tripped and either sprained or broke an ankle during a duck and cover alarm as they sprinted to the nearest yellow bunker.

As February became March, our three-man audit team endured a steady grind that, while appearing bearable on any given day, felt like a form of Chinese water torture. My routine consisted of waking up, walking to work, working, walking to lunch, walking back to work, working some more, walking to dinner, walking to the apartment, and, after that, passing time with a computer, TV, book, or phone, and then going to bed. Though I felt fortunate to have pleasant people as coworkers, even the nicest people can become burdensome when there's no opportunity to break free. Our living arrangement resembled the isolation of a small college campus in winter, except that the inhabitants were older & dustier and the music had a decidedly different ring.

As a native of upstate New York and a resident of Northern Virginia, I was accustomed to frequent outdoor recreation. Perhaps this is why the claustrophobic NEC environment drove me slowly but steadily into a state of depression. I was literally surrounded by work at all times.

After a typical stressful day I'd head to the DFAC for dinner, hoping for the solace of a conversation about home. Instead, my usual dining companion would be some senior management officer or former ambassador who was sure to ask questions about my auditing progress. This place was worse than *Hotel California*. Not only couldn't I leave, I couldn't even check out!

As the months wore on, depression and sleep deprivation began getting the better of me. Herb noticed that I wasn't my normal self and he suggested that I see the Embassy psychiatrist, who made frequent trips to

Baghdad from his base in Jordan. He also gave me the email address of the doctor's scheduler, because appointments were made in advance due to his packed schedule.

I responded by saying, "Well, don't only crazy people see a psychiatrist?"

Herb patiently replied that he himself had seen the psychiatrist for help with his own anxiety, and he was now feeling a lot better. After a flash of embarrassment for ignorantly implying something negative about Herb, I realized that he had done me a huge favor by removing the stigma of a psychiatrist from my own mindset. I took Herb's advice.

Dr. David Brinton was completely different from what I had imagined a psychiatrist to be. He looked like a triathlon athlete: super-fit, shaved bald, energized, and humorous. It was a pleasure to speak with him, and he assured me that I wasn't crazy because the stress I felt was situational. Also, I was not alone in my plight. In fact, when I mentioned my sleeping problems, he told me that about 50% of Embassy residents were suffering from sleep disorders.

While I didn't wish discomfort on anyone, this news came as a huge relief to me. It was great to have someone to talk with who understood what I was going through. Dr. Brinton prescribed some medication to help me sleep at night and I walked out feeling, if not better, at least *normal*.

Contact Has Been Made

March 2009

Confinement affects different people in different ways. Some take to drink, some watch movies, some have temporary marriages, and some turn to their faith. I fell into the latter category and found that the weekly chapel services offered salvation in a very practical way.

One day Robin introduced me to a Jordanian-born Arab interpreter named Jabil, who led a bilingual Arab-English Bible study for Iraqi Christians. These were not just any Christians, but MBBs – that is, Muslim-Background Believers.

I learned that MBB Christians could be – and often were – killed by Muslims, in accordance with Sharia, which is also known as Islamic Law. As Muhammad declared repeatedly in the hadiths,[15]

> *It is not permissible to take the life of a Muslim..., but in one of the three cases: 1. the married adulterer, 2. a life for life, and 3. the deserter of his Din (Islam), abandoning the {Islamic} community.*[16]

---

15 The Hadiths are traditional accounts of things said or done by Muhammad or his companions.

16 Sahih Muslim, Book 16, Number 4152. Similar hadiths can be found in *Sahih Bukhari*, Volume 9, Book 83, Number 17, and *Sahih Muslim*, Book 16, Numbers 4153, 4154, and 4155. See www.usc.edu/org/cmje/religious-texts/hadith/muslim/016-smt.php. This command is repeated in similar form throughout the hadiths.

The courage of these believers impressed me, and I wondered how many Christians back home would hold up under this kind of oppression. Needless to say I gladly accepted when Jabil invited Robin and me to join the group.

We arrived at the appointed time and found Jabil with a group of eight people. One of the MBB women had brought a complete Iraqi dinner to our gathering for all of us.

The food was delicious. This woman had brought freshly baked pita bread, rice, eggplant, curried chickpeas, and a roasted chicken that was so fresh that it must have been running in the henhouse earlier that day. We also ate pickled mangos in curry sauce – the only dish that didn't translate well to my American palate. Robin and I ate so much food so quickly that the Iraqi woman probably thought the Embassy was starving us.

After dinner we held our Bible study and sang hymns. It was beautiful to hear the Iraqis' praising God and singing in Arabic.

After months of isolation, the spirituality of the evening made me feel that I had finally connected with some Iraqis. Sadly, this sense of belonging made it especially hard to return to the monotony and boredom of life at the Embassy. It was also difficult to see Iraqis reaching out to us in friendship while knowing that Iraq's political situation kept us almost completely separated.

Robin later told me how she came to know Jabil and his group of MBB Christians:

> Before organizing the worship service at the Embassy, Robin had attended a service at Camp Union. After that service there was another one for MBB Iraqi Christians. Robin decided to stick around to see what it was like and possibly get to know some Iraqis. After listening to incomprehensible Arabic for a few minutes, she turned to go, but as she reached the door she suddenly heard something that made her stop in her tracks. The Iraqis had started singing the contemporary worship songs of Michael W. Smith – in English! Robin realized that these were people she could talk with and decided to introduce herself after the service.

Over the course of their conversation Robin learned that most of these MBB Christians were interpreters working for the military or the State Department, with security passes that provided access to the Green Zone and Camp Union. These passes were precious to them because they gave access to the only safe place where they could meet: the little hooch chapel in Camp Union. Prior to the Green Zone's existence it had been forbidden for these MBB Christians to worship Jesus publicly and even dangerous for them to gather together in private.

After starting our worship services at the NEC, Robin brought them to the Embassy on several occasions for services with her friends. Their gratitude for having new companions with whom they could safely share their testimonies and concerns was immense. All of us knew that, beyond the bounds of the Green Zone, these Christians had to live in secret and under the threat of death.

After returning from dinner, I called my Mom, a devout Christian, to tell her about the remarkable evening I had had with Robin and the Iraqi Christians. As I described the food they had prepared for us, The Big Voice suddenly came on and I had to cut our call short with what was becoming a standard phrase:

"Gotta go – ROCKET ATTACK!"

I threw on my PPE and ducked into the windowless dining room to await the all-clear signal with Richard, who was a few steps ahead of me.

Vacation in Jordan

April 2009

Richard, Herb, and I had been scheduled to spend a week in April at our boss's Amman office for some meetings and additional training. Recognizing that this trip would also be an escape from Iraq's tight security rules, I arranged for a second week there and got tickets for Ping to join me on a tour of Jordan.

Part of the surrealism of my job was the quick shifts we'd make from traumatic issues, such as bombings and kidnappings, to bureaucratic paper work or fun with our families. However it was impossible to be completely successful with these mental acrobatics, as I discovered during this vacation with Ping. In one sense I was away from the battle, but in another I had become aware of a *hidden* conflict, raging almost everywhere we went but concealed behind a facade of civility and tradition.

In the months since we had arrived in Iraq the flights between Baghdad and Amman hadn't improved; in fact they had gotten worse. To save money, those spacious and speedy C-17s had been replaced by relatively small and slow C-130s that used old-style red cargo netting for seats.

The C-130 nearly doubled the length of our flight to Amman, where we landed in the early afternoon after two hours in the air. The human cargo disembarked tenderly, thanks to modern-day saddle sores induced by the flight.

After arriving at our hotel I called Hertz and arranged for a driver to pick me up in a few hours. The plan was for him to take me to the Queen Aliya Airport so I could be there when Ping landed. However I soon discovered that even simple and clear instructions could be completely misunderstood – or ignored – in this part of the world.

The driver neither picked me up nor told me of any change in plans. Thankfully he still went to the airport, got Ping, and dropped her off at the hotel as I paced in the lobby wondering what happened. It was such a relief to see her again!

Ping and I hadn't seen each other for more than three months – our longest time apart since our wedding. As I waited for her I wondered whether our relationship would still be the same. It felt as if I had just arrived from a different planet, and I feared that she might feel the same way. Fortunately we enjoyed a beautiful dinner and evening together, and our apprehensions disappeared with the sunset.

Because I had a week of work to do before we could start our vacation, Ping had to find a way to keep busy during the day. Being adventurous, she decided to go sightseeing on her own.

While some people might not have been eager to explore a Middle-Eastern city alone, Ping went right to it. Fortunately she wasn't as alone as it appeared because I already knew the city and could give her useful tips in the morning and during our daily lunches together. With the aid of her fearless spirit she'd grab a taxi and visit places like Amman's Roman Theater, the Citadel, and the shopping bazaars.

Amman's U.S. Embassy was in an exclusive part of the city called Abdun. Wealthy Gulf natives preferred to invest in Jordan for its relative stability and liberal social environment, and Abdun was one of the key beneficiaries.

Among Abdun's amenities were a luxurious shopping district and a residential area filled with expansive mansions. Many of these mansions had small yards with grass and flowers – a welcome alternative to the heaps of litter and garbage we saw elsewhere. Abdun's cuisine was expensive but tasty and its restaurants exuded a pleasant and relaxing ambiance. Ping and I frequently had lunch there during that first week.

On Richard's and my first workday we took a taxi from our hotel to the Embassy. When the taxi arrived, Richard looked at the smudged and nearly unreadable taxi meter and asked, "JD14 or JD1.4?" Without hesitation the driver answered in English, "JD14" (US$21).

We thought that this price was exorbitant but figured that it might reflect Abdun's higher standard of living. We gave the driver JD15 and told him to keep the extra as a tip. Later we discovered that the fare was indeed JD1.4 and the driver had purposely ripped us off by charging ten times the going rate. Our tip had been nearly the value of the fare!

Upon exiting the taxi we saw a long line of people winding around the Embassy building. At the start of the line a sign said, "American Visa Section." Later that day I asked my boss about the long line. He replied, "Oh yeah, it's always like that when the Visa Consular Section is open to the public." Apparently the U.S. was a very popular destination.

The second week belonged to Ping and me, so we decided to rent a car and ramble through the countryside visiting Jordan's tourist spots.

Having driven in China, with its millions of new drivers and an infrastructure struggling to keep up with them, I figured that Jordan couldn't be any worse. I figured wrong.

A person can learn a lot about a place by driving in it, and Jordan reconfirmed this fact in a gut-wrenching way. Never before had I considered driving to be a true life-or-death experience.

Twice we were at a stoplight where a mother and her children were on the crosswalk in front of us. The instant the light turned green, the drivers behind us began blasting their horns and yelling angrily. I looked in my rear-view mirror and could see them shaking their fists and glaring at us because we hadn't moved immediately. Apparently they wanted us to run down whoever was in front of us.

There was also a time when we were driving slightly above the speed limit and the driver behind us began flashing his lights and honking his horn. I winked at Ping and told her that he must be trying to tell us that something's wrong with our car. Then I slowed down and turned on the flashers.

The Jordanian driver reacted by pulling up beside me and flailing his arms, his face glaring in furious rage. After several more near-altercations I determined that physical violence was a real possibility. This was not exactly what Ping and I had intended for our vacation so we decided to hire a driver on our next excursion.

Aside from the driving, though, we had a wonderful time. Our main destination was the ancient Roman city of Jerash, located about an hour-and-a-half north of Amman. The road leading to the site gave an impressive view of this well-preserved city, which was nearly unchanged after more than two thousand years. With so many buildings, temples and marble-colonnaded streets still standing, along with a nearly intact Roman coliseum, we felt like time-travelers. Jerash and its ancient remnants of Western civilization are a must-see for anyone who visits Jordan.

After reaching the hotel that night I explained our harrowing experience to Abdullah, the manager who had befriended us. He replied that driving in Jordan wasn't all that bad; it was much worse in Lebanon and Syria! As we stared back incredulously, he suggested that perhaps we had just been unlucky. With this assurance we hesitantly decided to try driving by ourselves at least one more time.

The goal of our second day was to visit the Islamic Ajlun Castle. According to our map, the way to this castle was well-marked and only about fifteen miles from Jerash. However we quickly learned that the highway exit signs might as well have said, "Abandon all hope, ye who enter here." In fact, for all we knew, this *was* what the signs said because they were all in Arabic. As we bewailed our sin of pridefully shunning a GPS system, the roads swirled in strange directions and mysteriously stopped. Though we often saw the elusive castle, standing majestically on a hill, we could never reach it. It was evident that a great chasm had been set between us, and we were numbered among the lost.

After two hours of futile wandering, I finally listened to my wife and pulled into a gas station for directions. A man in rags, with about three teeth, came up and asked how he could help us. To our surprise he spoke perfect English and provided helpful directions that quickly brought us to the Castle entrance.

The Ajlun Castle had an impressive view of the surprisingly green countryside. Far off in the distance we could see the Sea of Galilee as a beckoning dash of blue.

This castle was a rarity because it hadn't been built by Crusaders. Instead it had been built by Izz al-Din Usama, nephew of the great Saladin, to protect his territory from Crusader incursions. In those ancient times

Crusader strongholds were close by – in Karak to the south and in Basin to the west – making this castle a necessary defense.

The next stop on our itinerary was Um Qais, a site near the Israeli border whose famous Roman ruins overlooked the Sea of Galilee. According to the map it should have been easy to find, but we got hopelessly lost again and had to give up.

While we may not have reached our destination, this didn't mean that our trip was a disappointment.

As we drove, the major road we were on narrowed and eventually reduced to dirt, making it clear that we were completely off the tourist track. Realizing that we were on the verge of becoming hopelessly lost again, I stopped the car in what looked like the middle of nowhere to review our map and search for landmarks. My efforts were futile, though, because the only things in sight were some small rustic townhouses to our left and a gnarly old olive grove to our right.

At this point Ping and I realized that we were not going to see Um Qais that day, so we decided to take a tour of the local terrain, which had obviously seen few foreigners. As we looked over the rocky desert-like scene in the baking sun, we noticed that one of the more dilapidated townhouses had a porch with a group of children in its shade, munching a midday snack. They smiled and waved to us, so we decided to walk over and strike up a conversation with them.

The oldest was a girl who looked about twelve, and she identified the others as her brothers and sisters. Incredibly, she spoke English just as fluently as the old man. When we asked how she had learned to speak English so well, she replied, "at my school." Linguistically, at least, the Middle East was far more Americanized than we had ever imagined.

Unfortunately this Americanization meant that I wasn't very interesting to the kids. When the girl asked where we were from and I told her, "The United States," she responded with an unimpressed "Oh."

Then Ping mentioned that she was from China. Upon this news the girl perked up and told the others in excited tones. The children's eyes widened into saucers.

"Ahhhhhhh!...Oooooooh!"

It was as if Ping had just landed from Mars. The children suddenly wanted to know all about her and how we met each other and ended up in Jordan. We had a wonderful time telling them a few stories of our travels, with the oldest girl translating our words for the others. This chance encounter turned out to be the highlight of our day.

After a very pleasant conversation, Ping and I realized that it would be a good idea for us to retrace our way back to the hotel before it got dark. Before leaving, though, we asked the children whether we could take some pictures with them. This was another cause for excitement because they could see themselves in the digital camera's screen. Finally, the two of us loaded into our car and waved to the children as we drove back to Amman.

On our third morning we finally admitted that our driving skills were hopeless and returned to the Hertz office at our hotel to hire a driver. Omar was his name, and he identified himself as a Muslim Palestinian, which was curious because he later told us that he was born and raised in Jordan. As we darted along he also explained that Jordan's population was over 40% Palestinian. What struck me was that even though the majority of these people were Jordanian citizens, they did not see themselves that way. The American concept of a melting pot apparently didn't have much cachet over here.

Omar had met us at the hotel and drove us to the town of Madaba, which was about an hour from Amman. Madaba had a large Christian population (35%) and several well-known churches, one of which we decided to visit.

St. George's was a Greek Orthodox Church built in the 1800s on the site of an ancient Byzantine church. It was famous for its ancient Byzantine mosaic of Jerusalem, which was still clearly visible on the floor after fifteen hundred years.

Wandering among the ancient artifacts was a powerful spiritual experience. As we walked we found ourselves immersed in the church's fifteen centuries of history. A sense of awe filled us as we imagined the millions of souls who had walked along its venerable aisles.

The church had a wonderful guide, a Christian named Michel who loved St. George's more than any tourist could fully comprehend. He gladly offered to escort us around its grounds and buildings. As we walked, he provided a fascinating history lesson, explaining the ancient mosaics as we went.

As our tour ended I asked Michel whether there was freedom of religion in Jordan, and he confirmed that Jordan did indeed have freedom of worship. That was when I overstepped an invisible boundary. After witnessing a beautiful baptism ceremony, I gushed, "This place is so wonderful. I can really feel the Lord's presence here. It's so important for us to share the Good News..."

My voice trailed off as the expression on Michel's face darkened and became very serious. He told me that Christians mustn't witness to Muslims. When I asked why, he explained that someone (like the convert) could die, and that the evangelizer might lose his job or face other consequences.

Dismayed but not surprised (because of my experiences in Iraq), I replied that this didn't sound like freedom of religion to me. He replied that "freedom of worship" in Jordan was different from my concept of freedom of religion. Sadly, his description of Jordanian religious tolerance sounded more like resentfully putting up with backward tribes than anything having to do with genuine respect. It was also clear that this "tolerance" could evaporate in a heartbeat if the status quo was even remotely threatened.

Michel told us that he knew of MBB Christians in Jordan who had lost their lives simply because they converted to Christianity. While I was already aware of such murders, this news was a disturbing wakeup call for Ping about the true nature of Jordan's supposedly tolerant and secular society. Beneath a veil of pleasantry lay deep undercurrents of hostility and fear.

I later learned that, in the Islamic world, "religious tolerance" has a very different meaning from what we understand in the West. It means that Islamic society allows non-Muslims to exist, as long as the non-Muslims accept a second-class dhimmi[17] status. If non-Muslims "know their place" and don't call attention to themselves or their religions, they are more-or-less left alone.

However, non-Muslims find it difficult to get jobs or advance their careers. Also, if a non-Muslim has a dispute with a Muslim and goes to court, he or she will discover that a Muslim's testimony is considered superior to

---

17 A dhimmi is one of the "protected people," that is, a non-Muslim tolerated under the Sharia law of an Islamic state. This status, which was formalized under Umar, the 3rd "rightly guided" caliph to lead the Muslims after Muhammad's death, allows non-Muslims to live relatively unharassed in exchange for an annual poll tax called the jizya. However, Dhimmis also face significant disabilities. For example, they may be prohibited from owning weapons, they may not be allowed to strike back if struck by a Muslim, they may not evangelize to Muslims, and their testimony is considered inferior to that of a Muslim's in a court of law.

a non-Muslim's. All the Muslim has to do is swear by Allah and the judge will overrule anything contradictory the non-Muslim says. Given these terms of "toleration," it occurred to me that a more accurate word would be "discrimination."

It seemed remarkable that so many Christians were putting up with this bad treatment in Jordan and other parts of the Islamic world. However a little research helped me understand that Jordan, Syria, Egypt, Turkey, Libya, Tunisia, and Algeria had all once been heartlands of Christianity, and that Jordan had been 20% Christian only a hundred years ago. The Christians who remained came from long-declining populations whose members emigrated to the West in a steady stream to escape oppression. Only poverty or the cherished memories of places like St. George's kept the remainder from leaving.

As bad as this so-called "toleration" sounded, I recognized that it was less foreign than we Americans would like to think. Those of us with long memories can still recall an era in the United States when African Americans endured similar forms of oppression. The phrase "Separate but equal" and Harper Lee's *To Kill a Mockingbird* are lasting testimonies to an ugly past.

However there *was* a difference between what happened in the United States and what I saw in Jordan and Iraq. While the U.S. could not escape the accusation of once being little better than Jordan, we also knew that our nation had left those bad old days behind it, as Herb could attest. Our core beliefs in freedom and equal justice opposed the institutions of segregation and discrimination, and ultimately defeated them. Today such injustice is unthinkable. On the other hand, I didn't see how we could expect the same triumph to happen among people whose religion requires dhimmitude of non-Muslims.

After saying a prayer and giving Michel a donation for St. George's Church, we returned to Omar, who had been waiting outside. I decided to keep my moving faith experience to myself as we set off to the next stop on our route: Mount Nebo.

For the next half-hour we drove across a vast and desolate landscape. This made Mt. Nebo, at 3,300 feet above sea level, all the more impressive when we finally got to it and saw its beautiful ancient mosaics. On the platform at the summit there was a modern Italian sculpture depicting Moses' staff and Jesus' words: "As Moses lifted up the serpent in the wilderness, so must the Son of Man be lifted up" – John 3:14.[18] The feelings that came over me as I stood where Moses once beheld the Promised Land were incredible.

Ping, who was more of an iconoclast, commented that the Promised Land didn't look very promising to her; instead it looked more like a dry, barren desert. I responded that, after wandering in the wilderness of the Sinai for forty years, just about anything would probably look like paradise. Also, the valleys might have been greener three thousand years ago. Later, I investigated this question and discovered that climate researchers believe the land had indeed been wetter once. They also believe that primitive farming methods had contributed to the region's loss of fertility. Amazingly, Israel has been able to reverse this trend in recent years and turned many of the former deserts green.

The museum at Mount Nebo held a remarkable collection of Byzantine mosaics and other artifacts, connecting us intimately with people from more than 1500 years ago. The images in the tiles, their cool touch, and even their faint odors beckoned to us and recalled a once-glorious but lost civilization.

After Mount Nebo, we took Omar's advice and pulled into a nearby buffet restaurant for lunch. Apparently it belonged to a friend of his. This restaurant swirled with smoke, flies, and the pungent aroma of questionable food.

While we ate, Omar went over to talk with his friend. When he returned, the urgency in his bulging eyes told us that we should have paid more attention to the clock. Minutes later we were racing at nearly 100 mph to our next destination: Bethany Beyond the Jordan. Ping and I exchanged hushed words in the back seat, imagining a rescue squad prying us from our wrecked vehicle. As we flew along, the accountant in me couldn't help but wonder, "Does our insurance cover third-party drivers?"

In a remarkably short time we found ourselves at the parking lot of one of the reputed sites of Jesus' baptism. Before we could even open our doors, Omar had jumped out and approached the person at the ticket counter. Apparently we had arrived just as the very last tour of the day was departing. While we didn't have a second to spare, we made it thanks to Omar's fast action.

---

18   See www.sacred-destinations.com/jordan/mount-nebo.htm.

Bethany Beyond the Jordan lay near the Dead Sea, more than a thousand feet below sea level. It looked like Death Valley with a somewhat larger stream. Although it was only April, the temperature was already in the 90s and the humidity was about zero.

Having come from Baghdad, I felt comfortable in this kind of weather. Ping, on the other hand, had only recently arrived from the cool humidity of Virginia's springtime and she was not adapting well. In fact, she looked like she was turning into a mummy. Despite her discomfort, she tried her best to avoid complaining, realizing how important this moment was for me. There was no way she could control the raspy sensation in her throat, though. As we walked, she would periodically choke out gasps of "I can't breathe!" while urgently raising a bottle of water to her parched lips.

Ping was a saint for quietly enduring that two-mile desert hike to the Jordan River's shores. As I watched her struggle so stoically, I knew that at some point my day of reckoning would come. Sure enough, when I returned home in July, she handed me a long honey-do list, and I was just as stoic when I went through chore after chore for her.

The first stop of our tour was the reputed site of Jesus' baptism. It was a small spring where ancient steps led from the remains of a 5th century Byzantine Church. The reason we saw a spring instead of a river was that the Jordan had shrunk over the past two thousand years and was now sixty meters away.

Our next stop was the River itself. It actually looked more like the small creek behind our home in Virginia than the mighty landmark described in the Bible.

I walked to its shore and dipped my fingers into its water. Why just my fingers? We had been forewarned that the Jordan was very polluted. Any greater exposure could be harmful.

On the opposite bank and about thirty meters away was the *other* claimed Baptism site of Jesus, enclosed in a white concrete building and surrounded by a large open porch. Directly in front was a series of steps or seats where people could sit behind a chest-high metal fence. Below the fence was a fifteen-foot tan stone wall that dropped directly into the Jordan River, with an opening whose steps led to the water.

Flying overhead was the Israeli flag with its Star of David. I had dreamt of seeing the Promised Land since childhood, and here we were, standing just meters away from it. Tears began to well up as I cracked with emotion.

After this visit we walked back to the hot and dusty open-air shuttle bus and returned to the parking lot. Ping was gasping and wheezing the whole way and I began to worry about her getting heat exhaustion. Although Ping didn't suffer from any chronic condition, her body was clearly unprepared for the desert climate and seemed to be reacting in much the same way as mine did when I first arrived in Baghdad. Fortunately, once we returned to the comfort of our air-conditioned rental car, Ping's gasps turned into a big sigh of relief. She may have had to deal with the dry heat outside, but not the lingering effects of Baghdad's pollution and dust.

After enduring all of this discomfort for my sake, Ping finally got to see a place that she had longed to visit since she was a small girl in China: the Dead Sea.

The road to the Dead Sea was among the most barren and desolate we'd ever seen, and the temperature, if anything, was even hotter than at the baptismal site. The hostile and salty landscape was devoid of plant life, but the views of the sea were spectacular.

Our first stop was the Dead Sea Public Beach. Omar pulled into a parking lot so that Ping and I could step out and look around. We got out of the car, walked to the top of the beach, and then stared at each other in disgust.

If someone had told us that we were visiting a landfill we would have believed it. We had never seen so much garbage on a beach in our lives, not even after a hurricane. There were bottles, dirty diapers, plastic bags, car batteries, Styrofoam cups, and paper plates everywhere we looked. Vandals couldn't have trashed this beach any more than the locals who used it. It was awful, and we weren't sure why Omar even took us there. However, we kept our thoughts to ourselves and told him that we were ready to continue to our destination: the Dead Sea Marriott.

On the way, we saw two Bedouin tribesmen leading several large camels on a leash and offering rides to tourists. It looked like fun, so we decided to give it a try.

I should have known by then that, in Jordan, everything revolved around money, and tourists were prime targets for opportunists. However we again made the mistake of not first asking those charming Bedouin what they charged. Now it was Ping's turn to discover Jordan's custom of fleecing tourists.

After our ride Omar asked the Bedouin what we owed. Their conversation soon became loud and I could tell that Omar was getting upset. He came back and told us that they wanted JD50 (US$75) for our 5-minute camel ride. I became incensed and told them that this was nonsense. The Bedouin became belligerent and Ping tensed up, fearing for her safety.

I asked Ping to go back to the car and then told Omar that I wasn't going to give them more than JD10. At that point one of the Bedouin got right into my face, making his bad breath another experience I will never forget.

For a minute I thought the situation would get physical, but when Omar and I spun around and walked back to the car they didn't follow us. Later we found out that the JD10 we paid was still double the going rate.

Poor Omar, who was so proud of his country! He was shaken by this experience and he apologized profusely, saying that this wasn't the real Jordan. I told him not to worry about it and assured him that Ping and I knew that good and bad people could be found everywhere in the world.

As we continued through the desert we saw a distant oasis of green that soon became the Dead Sea Marriott. With its lush tropical gardens, manicured landscaping, fruit trees, and swimming pools, it was refreshingly different from our other experiences that day.

While the Marriott was beautiful, even here we had to get used to the local peculiarities. For example we wondered why there were several cats slinking through the restaurant as we ate our breakfast buffet. What were they looking for? We hoped it was just table scraps. We gave them the evil eye as they contemplated jumping on our table.

After we finished breakfast with our feline friends, we returned to the hotel lobby, where we heard some strangely familiar sounds:

"Hot, eh?"

"For sure! For sure!"

To our surprise we discovered that the hotel was teeming with Canadians. Fortunately I managed to fit right in, having spent nearly every summer of my life at the old family cottage in Ontario. We discovered from our conversation with a Canadian diplomat's wife that the Canadian

Embassies of Saudi Arabia and Jordan were hosting a one-week conference on facilitating immigration to Canada.

The Canadian diplomats were staying in $250 per night hotel rooms and eating from the finest buffets. Aside from our northerly neighbors, the other patrons were primarily Arabs, with a smattering of Europeans. As far as we could tell, we were the only guests from the United States.

When we awoke the next morning Ping jumped right out of bed. After so many years of wishing, she was finally going to float on the Dead Sea!

The Dead Sea is famous for being one of the saltiest lakes on the planet.[19] What makes it so salty is the fact that it lies at the lowest point on the Earth's surface, 1,388 feet below sea level. Water flows *in* through the Jordan River and other tributaries, but it doesn't flow *out*. All it can do is evaporate, leaving its dissolved salt and other minerals behind. Water from the Dead Sea has a salinity of 33%, about 8.6 times the saltiness of ocean water.

We soon discovered that this wonder of the natural world had more in store for us than met the eye – literally. In addition to its stunning scenery, it also offered unforgettable lessons on following instructions.

I had been forewarned, "DO NOT SHAVE!" before going into the Sea, but I did so anyway to look good for the photos. I was soon to learn how big mistakes can appear innocuous to an unsuspecting tourist.

We walked across the stony beach and prepared for the famous float. As I eased into the water, a few drops lapped onto my face and neck. Instantly a surge of pain rushed over me like a swarm of angry bees. I was grateful when the stinging soon disappeared, but it drove home the point that this water was *different*.

We had suspected that this water was different from the moment we stepped into it because it felt like warm maple syrup, despite its crystal clarity. My stinging face taught me *how* different it was.

Stepping further into the sea transformed us into corks as we felt our bodies being pushed up by the heavy water. Then we tipped back and… Whoops! Our legs swung up and we began floating effortlessly on top of the water's surface. While we still had to move our hands occasionally, this was only to prevent the wind from blowing us out to sea.

---

19 Only two lakes are saltier: Antarctica's Don Juan Lake is the saltiest, and Djibouti's Lake Assal, is the second saltiest.

Ping's lesson on following instructions was slightly different from mine. She had lost her balance when she tipped back and splashed slightly. That's when she found out why the hotel staff told us, "NEVER NEVER SPLASH!" A single drop of water touched her left eyelid, and as she blinked the tiniest amount of water seeped into the corner of her eye. This fraction of a drop was enough to cause searing pain. Fortunately she recovered after a few minutes and we both ended up having a wonderful time bobbing around with the other tourists.

The Dead Sea is also famous for its therapeutic mud, reputed to be good for the skin despite what we had been told about the Jordan River's pollution. The hotel got its mud from further down the coast and trucked it up in large bins. Guests would dip their hands into the mud and then slap it all over their bodies, letting it dry into a very hard shell. After about ten minutes, the guests would wade into the Dead Sea to wash it off.

Another rule we learned – fortunately not the hard way – was to NEVER spend more than fifteen minutes in the Dead Sea. We were warned that after fifteen minutes certain parts of the anatomy would get very sore.

This was one warning that needed no reminder. In fact, anyone soaking in the Dead Sea quickly got the urge to jump out and shower off because the salt was crystallizing everywhere imaginable.

The next morning, while Ping was getting her mud facial and massage, I decided to go for a swim in one of the Marriott's pools. It turned out to be bouncing with gorgeous women in skimpy bikinis.

I thought to myself that these must be European women, because Muslim women would *never* dress like this. When I heard them speaking in Arabic, I thought, "Perhaps they're Arab Christians..."

With curiosity getting the better of me, I decided to investigate and began a conversation with three of the ladies. After a while I asked whether they were Muslim and they answered together, "Oh yes, we're Muslim." After all of the pious clothing I had seen elsewhere, this conversation left my head spinning. It seemed like the more I learned about Islamic culture the more bewildered I got.

After three sunny and relaxing days at the Dead Sea Marriott we headed off to Petra. On the way, Omar took us by the Dead Sea Panoramic Complex, located on top of a mountain whose peak was actually at sea level. Once again the views were spectacular.

Following lunch we drove to Lot's Cave, the reputed spot where Lot lived with his daughters for two years after God destroyed Sodom and Gomorrah. Then we took a side-trip to Karak Castle – another impressive Crusader monument.

By the end of the tour it was getting late, so we decided to drive to the modern town of Petra and check in at the Petra Marriott. The next morning Omar took us to the entrance of the adjacent original city. Historic Petra was by far the most remarkable ancient site in Jordan, earning its reputation as one of the New Seven Wonders of the World.

Historic Petra was first built in about 100 BC as the trading center and capital of the Nabataeans. They were once a loosely-connected society of traders whose appearance in the historical record followed the Jew's Babylonian exile, apparently helping to fill a power vacuum. Petra became a Nabataean trading center when they mastered the art of capturing the wintry rainy season's water in Petra's rocks. For the rest of the year, thirsty caravans came from afar to buy the water stored in Petra's huge hidden cisterns, turning this man-made oasis into a wealthy trading center.

The tombs, monasteries, and coliseums of this ancient city extended for miles into the desert, creating a sense of vastness that impresses even today. Surveying these ruins, we wondered in awe at what it must have been like when it was a vibrant city, before an earthquake cracked the cisterns and drained the city's water supply in 363 AD.

After a half-mile trek, we saw a massive cistern that resembled a cavern carved into the rock. Like the hundreds of smaller cisterns that peppered the area, it was well camouflaged to avoid detection by foreign interlopers.

This cistern was about a half-mile long, after which it became an opening into the Treasury, a structure that gained its name from a legend that bandits once hid their treasure in an urn high on its second floor. The Treasury was a massive building, again carved into solid rock, whose original purpose is a mystery. However it had found a new purpose in recent history as one of the most popular photo-ops in Petra, made famous by its starring role in *Indiana Jones and the Temple of Doom*.

Everywhere in Petra we saw giant carvings, tombs, and other impressive structures, all cut from living rock, along with temples, colonnades, and a Nabataean coliseum. The quality of this ancient city's preservation was nearly as amazing as the city itself.

By late afternoon we had walked and climbed ourselves to exhaustion and were ready for a break. However when I looked at our map I noticed that we hadn't yet seen the Monastery – the second-most impressive site in Petra. The only problem was that we had to climb 800 steps to reach the top of the mountain where it sat. Realizing that we may never get this opportunity again, we ignored our aching legs and began the ascent.

On the way we noticed a group of girls dressed in soccer jerseys. I started a conversation with one of them and discovered that they were a girls' soccer team from Jeddah, Saudi Arabia. They were in Jordan to play a match with their Jordanian counterparts and had decided to do some sightseeing while they were there.

After a few more questions we discovered that the team leader, Aalia, had lived in McLean, Virginia for two years. Her home had been only a few miles from ours and she often shopped at the mall next to Ping's workplace. What a small world! We posed for pictures and then continued our hike. I thought to myself about this first conscious encounter with Saudis and how friendly and normal they seemed. They were nothing like the alien beings swathed in black and accompanied by male guardians that we would have met in Saudi Arabia itself, assuming that the guardians would have allowed us to meet them.

Finally we reached step number 800 and the mountain leveled into a plateau about 100 yards wide. On the opposite side stood the Monastery – another enormous columned structure carved into the rock and covered with elaborate details.

While the structure was impressive, we loved the quiet serenity of the location more than anything else. Far removed from the throngs of tourists and Bedouin vendors, we appreciated how this could be an ideal site for a monastery.

Returning down the mountain, the steps felt even more difficult than they did going up. Our brochure told us that the park closed at 5 PM, so we checked our watches and saw that it was 4:50 PM. We had ten minutes to hike several miles if we wished to leave on time!

Though we knew we couldn't make it we decided to do the best we could and hoped that we wouldn't get into trouble. As we finished our descent we noticed a teenage boy standing ahead of us holding two donkeys on a leash. When we reached him he asked whether we'd like a ride to the gate.

This time we wisely asked the price before giving him an answer. He responded with the usual 10X overcharge, so we declined and began to walk away. As if by magic the price instantly dropped to an acceptable amount and we agreed.

The boy's name was Muhammad. He was a very personable 16-year-old who spoke English, French, German, and a little Korean, which he picked up to attract various kinds of tourists. Ping asked Muhammad whether he went to school and he replied that he dropped out years ago to help support his nine brothers and sisters.

Finally, with the sun approaching the horizon, our donkey ride ended and we left the park. Apparently the gates only closed at 5 PM for *incoming* visitors, so our late departure wasn't a problem at all. We were sore and exhausted but also relieved. As we rode back to our hotel, we reminisced about the beautiful experiences we had that day and the memories we'll never forget.

When we arose the next morning we quickly checked out of the Petra Marriott, which had turned out to be a Motel 6 experience for a Ritz Carlton price. I concluded that Jordanians had to be very rich because everything was expensive compared to the U.S....at least for tourists who weren't used to bartering.

As usual, Omar, whom we had come to consider a friend, was punctually waiting for us in the lobby. We put our luggage in the car and began our journey back to Amman for Ping's flight home. We felt relaxed and tired, happy and sad. All too soon our time together was coming to an end.

On the way to the airport I noticed an enormous tree on the side of the road that had to be more than three hundred years old. I asked Omar if he could stop the car so we could get a better look at it.

Omar responded by veering directly into the driveway next to the tree. This felt a bit intrusive to us, especially when the owner and his son stepped out of the house to see what was going on. As they stared, Omar walked over to talk with them. We felt a little nervous, but after a few minutes Omar walked back and said that the family had invited us in for lunch. This was a very kind gesture, but with our eyes on Ping's departure we thanked them and declined the offer.

However we asked whether it was okay for us to look at the tree in their backyard. They quickly agreed and added that there were two more trees nearby, both of which were more than 900 years old. Wow! After taking pictures we returned to our car and continued to Amman.

Upon our arrival Omar dropped us off at the upscale Grand Hyatt Hotel, where Ping and I enjoyed a last romantic dinner together. As agreed, Omar met us again at the hotel that evening and drove us to the airport for Ping's flight back to the U.S. After we shared our good-byes and Ping departed, Omar and I returned to the hotel.

On the way we had a curious conversation. Omar had been telling me some interesting details about life in Jordan when he switched the subject to marriage. He told me that, though it wasn't common, Muslim men could take additional wives if, for example, one's current wife was diseased or unable to have children. I wondered to myself how a second wife would make the first wife feel. This was not an academic issue, because Ping and I had mentioned to him that we were childless.

Omar also shared some stories about his family and his children, especially his baby girl. He wanted to introduce us to them and made an open invitation for us to have dinner at his house whenever we returned to Jordan.

After spending five days with Omar, Ping and I felt that we had developed a genuine friendship with him. I felt this way even though it had become clear that we had some very different core values, and his discussion of children and second wives made me feel a bit uncomfortable. We simply saw the world differently. Like people on opposite sides of a chasm, we were close enough to speak but separated by a deep divide.

Two days later, and after some additional sightseeing on my own, another Hertz driver met me at the hotel. Soon I was journeying back to Marka Airport and life in Baghdad.

Iraq and Jordan Photos

Richard in Amman

Herb and me at the Republican Palace swimming pool

Helmet? Check! Bulletproof Vest? Check! Let the audit begin.

A helicopter's-eye view of Baghdad

Amman's old Roman Theater, with modern buildings in the background

Ajlun Castle

*Sitting with the children Ping and I met
on the porch of their townhouse*

A Baptism ceremony at St. George's Church

*The claimed site of Jesus' baptism in Jordan,
now a spring-fed pool instead of the Jordan River*

*Dipping my fingers into the
Jordan River in front of Israel's
claimed baptism site of Jesus*

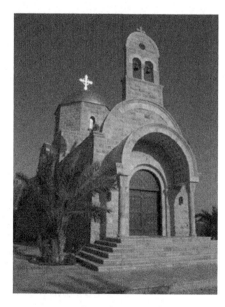

*A church near the
Jordanian Baptism pool*

Wading in the trash at the Dead Sea Public Beach

Ping's and my five-minute camel ride,
which nearly cost us $75

The Dead Sea Marriott

The Monastery at Petra

View from the July 14th Bridge

The Tomb of the Unknown Soldier

*One of the Crossed Swords monuments,
with T-walls in the background*

*The helmets of dead Iranians, cleared from the battlefields
of the Iran-Iraq War. Over the years, the looser helmets
had been scavenged, leaving craters in the concrete.*

New Mosque complex directly across the street from the Embassy

View of a Baghdad dust storm

The Kuwait Towers

Vice President Biden's visit to the Embassy

An Iraqi bullet-proof guard booth next to some low T-walls

Travel by C-130 feels good when you're going home!

The Presbyterian Church in Iraq

May 2009

One evening in early May I had dinner with two leaders of the Presbyterian Church: an Iraqi I'll call Naim and an American named Jim. Naim asked Jim and me to tell Americans back home about the plight of Iraq's Christians.[20]

"We are in great need of jobs!" cried Naim as he ravenously devoured his rib eye steak, courtesy of the Embassy. "We cannot support ourselves. All of the Christians who could get out of Iraq have left. Only the poorest ones remain."

Naim was a 60 year-old engineer with his own firm in Baghdad. He should have been thriving, given all of the new construction taking place. However Naim had one big problem: he was a Christian, and Christians didn't get work.

If he were Shiite or Sunni he would have been doing very well. "It's sort of an old boys' network with major religious backing," Naim confided with

---

20 This chapter is a joint account by a fellow Embassy employee (name withheld) who was very active in encouraging the Presbyterian Church in Iraq and helping Iraqi orphans during his non-working hours.

resignation. "Under Saddam everyone was the same. It didn't matter if you were Christian; all people were equal."

We could understand why Naim saw Saddam as a champion of equality. The changes in Iraq's religious climate over the preceding six years had been stark. Christians were suffering persecution as never before in Iraq's modern history.

We pressed Naim for more information with a barrage of questions: "Where do you live? Do you have children? A wife? How long have you been here?"

As Naim talked we discovered some common threads between his and Jim's experiences. It turned out they had both done rescue work after the Canal Hotel bombing of 2003, which killed twenty-two people and injured over a hundred.

The Canal Hotel had been the headquarters of the UN in Iraq. On August 19, 2003 a heavy truck packed with explosives blew off the western corner of the building and collapsed three floors.[21]

Naim's home was several blocks away but the blast still shattered his windows. As for Jim, he was standing next to his Blackhawk Helicopter about two and a half miles away when he first heard the blast. A few seconds later a shock wave shuddered through his body.

Naim had begun to panic as concerned phone calls poured in from his friends. They knew that his son was an IT specialist for the United Nations and that he had been in the building at the time.

Naim ran from his home to the smoldering ruins and began a frantic search for his son. Meanwhile Jim strapped into his Blackhawk helicopter and hurdled toward the biggest cloud of black smoke he'd ever seen. Their new shared mission was the rescue, security, and medical evacuation of victims.

Naim told us, "I searched for three hours and finally found my son trapped in a pocket of space under a collapsed floor. When I heard his voice I couldn't believe it. He was black from the smoke but I was so happy to see him alive!"

Our conversation expanded from this shared experience to that of the Presbyterian Church. As Secretary of the Iraqi Presbytery and moderator of the Baghdad Presbyterian Church Council, Naim was aware of all that was going on. He painted a tragic picture of the Church's recent history. In summary:

---

21   For more information, see http://en.wikipedia.org/wiki/Canal_Hotel_bombing .

The Presbyterian Church of Iraq had been established in 1820 when American missionaries first arrived in Nineveh. By 1840 Presbyterians had built the Baghdad Presbyterian Church, which was the one Naim attended. From there, Presbyterian churches also sprang up in Basrah, Kirkuk, and Mosul. In 1921 a second church called the Assyrian Presbyterian Church of Baghdad was built to accommodate Baghdad's growing Christian population.

While the churches thrived for many decades, conditions deteriorated after Saddam Hussein's overthrow. After that the Assyrian Presbyterian Church of Baghdad was shuttered by chronic violence, with most of its members fleeing to Jordan. Its six remaining families were transferred to Naim's church.

When we asked Naim how his church had held up, he replied that it once had 360 families back in 2003 but had been reduced to only 160, including the 6 transfers from the Assyrian Presbyterian church. While some members had been murdered, most had escaped to Jordan. However the remaining members were the poorest and least able to defend themselves. The only reason they remained in Baghdad was that they couldn't afford to leave.

He told us that pastors were hard to find as well, and the Baghdad church had just hired its first pastor since 2004. Apparently the anti-Christian violence was especially directed at church leaders and drove the previous pastor and elders out of the country. The terrorists knew that, by kidnapping and killing those at the top, they could terrorize entire congregations into leaving. In the wake of this diabolically successful strategy, the remaining families were left with the difficult task of reestablishing an entire administration by themselves. There were similar stories throughout the Presbytery.[22]

Naim told us, "Sixty percent of the people in our churches have left the country. If we do not find a way to get jobs there will be

---

22 Presbyterian polity is a method of church governance typified by the rule of assemblies of presbyters, or elders. Each local church is governed by a body of elected elders usually called the session. Groups of local churches are governed by a higher assembly of elders known as the presbytery; presbyteries can be grouped into a synod, and synods nationwide often join together in a general assembly.
See http://en.wikipedia.org/wiki/Presbytery_(church_polity)#The_Presbytery.

no more Christians in Iraq. Christians will be another part of Iraq's history, just as in Saudi Arabia."

Naim also told us about his cousin, Munthir: "In November of 2006, kidnappers took my cousin and held him several days for a million-dollar ransom. His family couldn't come up with the money so the kidnappers shot him in the head and dumped his body."

Munthir had been the chairman of the Mosul Presbyterian Church council. Apparently al-Qaeda in Iraq got wind of this information and decided to eliminate him as part of their general plan to kill Church leaders. After hearing of this brutal murder I was amazed that Naim hadn't fled with the rest of the leaders.

I later did some independent research on Munthir's death and confirmed it through a December 2006 article in *Asia News*:[23]

AsiaNews sources in Iraq confirmed the death of Elder Munthir, 69, a high-ranking leader of the Presbyterian Church in Mosul. Kidnapped on 26 November, the man's body four days later was found with a bullet in the skull, as recently reported by the Compass Direct news agency. This is the second kidnapping of a Christian from Mosul that has ended in tragedy in as many months. On 11 October, the body of Fr Paulos Eskandar was found. Fr Eskandar was a Syro-Orthodox priest who had been kidnapped two days earlier. According to anonymous sources in Mosul, the kidnappers of Munthir had demanded a ransom of one million dollars, adding threats like: "We will kill all Christians, starting with him."

This Presbytery had seen its share of insanity in recent years, but Jim told us that he felt fortunate to have been there for most of it. By "fortunate," Jim meant that it had been a faith-deepening blessing to encourage Iraqi brothers and sisters in Christ during their time of need. He felt blessed to have helped them hold onto their faith and bring dignity to the persecution they endured.

---

23 *Christian leader in Mosul kidnapped and killed*, December 12, 2006, Asia News, www.asianews.it/index.php?l=en&art=7937

As our meal came to an end I realized that these Christians were living as *true* martyrs, unlike those who claimed martyrdom while killing others. In their suffering they were demonstrating a faith as strong as that of the ancient apostles, clinging to Jesus' salvation in the face of rampant evil.

As we finished our dinner, Naim thanked us for our time and asked us to pray for his family and for the Presbyterian Church in Iraq. After we prayed together I promised him that I would do everything I could to help his community. That promise has weighed heavily on me ever since.

Working in a War Zone

June 2009

By June 2009 the Jordan vacation was a distant memory and I had sunken back into the normal routine of life at the Embassy. It had been four weeks since my colleague Herb had decided to resign and return home to be with his family. Life at the Embassy felt emptier now because Herb and I had become close, and his friendship had helped make life in Iraq bearable. I sorely missed his sense of humor and wise advice.

Between our pariah status as auditors and the reduction of our team from three to two, my sense of isolation was becoming unbearable. There were times when I neared my own breaking point and also contemplated quitting. On such days the aspects of life that were usually just dreary and distressing would culminate into a climax of misery.

For example, one particular day began with Iraq's signature weather event: a dust storm.[24] The soil in and around Baghdad was very sandy, but this sand in no way resembled the beautiful ribbons of bright color I remembered from Florida and the Bahamas. Instead, it was a dirty and powdery sand that got into everything, including teeth, eyes, hair, lungs, shoes, rugs, food, and paperwork. In fact, the sand was so powdery that it

---

24 The terms "dust storm" and "sandstorm" are used interchangeably.

behaved like dust, so that a "dust storm" was simply a "sand storm" whose winds weren't strong enough to kick up the larger grains of sand.

When I awoke that morning it was still dark, meaning that another sandstorm had arrived. I peered out the window looking for the Chancery building but couldn't see it through the haze. It was going to be another rough day.

Outside my bedroom window was an eerie brownish-orange scene, a grimy mutation of the whiteouts I remembered from my childhood days near Buffalo, NY. As I dressed for work, I made sure to leave my white shirts in the closet because anything white would be brownish by the end of the day. Then I stepped into the haze of dust that wafted slowly through the hallway. Every time someone entered or left the building, a little more dust floated in.

Once outside, conditions deteriorated rapidly. I could barely breathe and my eyes, which were too dry to make tears, were defenseless against the stinging dust. Then came the taste of the dust's fecal matter, which penetrated my mouth and coated my throat.

This fecal matter was such a problem that the Defense Department actually published a report on it entitled *Fecal Matter in the Air – What do we know?* [25] Therefore it was a great relief when, five long minutes later, I stepped into my workplace and basked in its excellent ventilation.

Sometimes these storms could last for hours. At other times they'd last for days or even weeks, as happened several times during my stay. Waking up to blue sky after a week-long sandstorm could feel like Christmas morning, or the end of a siege.

The 104-acre compound's confinement[26] made the Embassy a hothouse of cabin fever. Our only breaks from this hothouse were rare trips around the four square-mile Green Zone, which barely qualified as an improvement. I'd often find myself fantasizing about kayaking trips back home and other vacations I had always wanted. Any location was fine as long as it was far from the Middle East.

---

25   *Fecal Matter in the Air -- What do we know?*, March 2004, A Collaborative Effort of USACHPPM and AFIOH. This report can be found on-line at http://phc.amedd. army.mil/PHC%20Resource%20Library/AIR%20QUALITY%20-%20FECAL%20 MATTER%20FINAL%20Mar%2004.pdf

26   Of these 104 acres, only 67 of are accessible to regular employees.

Despite my prescription from the psychiatrist, I still suffered from insomnia. Try as I might, it was impossible to get a good night's sleep. This sleeplessness got steadily worse with time and would only abate during my trips back home or vacationing with Ping. In the familiar surroundings of my own bed, lying next to my wife, I could sleep like a baby, but once I was back in Iraq the insomnia was not far behind.

While my Embassy bed was not top-of-the-line, it was certainly comfortable enough, and noise was never a problem thanks to thick ballistic glass windows. In fact, except for the duck-and-cover alarms, I'd rarely even know about the exploding rockets that startled the contractors from sleep in their "soft" hooches. However the knowledge that we could come under attack at any time created an underlying tension that popped out in strange and unexpected ways. For example, there was a time when KBR's laundry service lost a pair of Richard's socks, and he really yelled at them about it. I thought that stress had finally gotten the better of Richard, as if he might not be able to handle our situation. A few weeks later I caught myself literally doing the exact same thing.

Adding to this stress was the nature of my Embassy work itself. An illustrative example is the case of an audit in which I was to meet with the Director of ITAO (the Iraq Transition and Assistance Office):

ITAO was responsible for reconstruction projects throughout Iraq, and it took weeks for them to slow down enough to even look at their calendars. Finally, after searching through six weeks of schedule conflicts, the Director and I found a date available for both of us.

On Memorial Day, two days before our meeting, disaster struck. An IED attack killed ITAO's Deputy Director, Terry Barnich, along with an Egyptian-American ACE (Army Corps of Engineers) named Dr. Maged Hussein. This was their reward for inspecting a new U.S.-built wastewater plant for the residents of Fallujah. Terry and Maged were two hardworking individuals dedicated to helping the Iraqis, but the terrorists decided that they had to die. Terry had left a high-profile career in the U.S. as the CEO of New Paradigm Resources to come to Iraq and make a positive difference while serving his country. His sacrifice turned out to be more than he ever imagined – *everything!*

The ITAO department fell apart in grief and my meeting became a part of the collateral damage, along with my entire audit. I couldn't help but think, "We've spent untold billions helping the Iraqis build schools, roads, sewage treatment and water plants, and this is how they thank us? No wonder Churchill called Iraq an 'ungrateful volcano'!"[27]

It took hard mental discipline to avoid blaming all Iraqis for the acts of the terrorists, but I knew that if I did, I'd be falling into another terrorist trap. I gritted my teeth and resolved not to let that physical bomb claim me as a psychological casualty by embittering me against those whom we served.

Two days later the DFAC closed early as the cafeteria staff began to prepare for the Terry Barnich and Maged Hussein Memorial Service. First they set up rows of chairs and decorated the room with flowers. Then they lovingly arranged pictures of Terry and Maged on a long table covered in blue cloth. Terry was fifty-six and Maged was forty-three. Maged left behind a wife and two young children. Although I never knew either of these individuals personally, I was still profoundly saddened by the loss.

A few weeks after the murders, there was one more casualty from the attack: I happened to walk by the ITAO department head's residence and noticed that it had been completely cleaned out, with her front door standing open. When I asked one the ITAO employees what happened, he told me that she had abruptly departed and returned home following the deaths. That's all I was told. That's all I'll ever know.

Fridays offered a rare weekly escape from the dreariness of Embassy life. This was the day one of my few friends, a young Embassy plumber named Trey, would join me for lunch at the Chinese restaurant across the street from the Embassy. The food wasn't bad, but our real reason for going was to escape the Embassy for a change of pace. Trey was the only American plumber I'd ever known who spoke Chinese, and the two of us had a great time practicing with the waitresses.

The restaurant employed two middle-aged Chinese waitresses who had come to Iraq for the same reason as most of the American civilians: to earn money for their families back home. But this was not why they stayed there.

---

27 *Winston S. Churchill IV, Companion Volume Part 3*, By Martin Gilbert, London: Heinemann, 1977, page 1974.

After we all got to know each other, they confided something to us that left us both in shock. Speaking in Chinese for privacy, they told us that the restaurant's Iraqi owner had seized their passports and was holding one of them against her will.

When I suggested that this woman should contact the Chinese Embassy for help, she replied that she had but the embassy refused to act. As appalling as this was, we had no control over the behavior of the Iraqi businessman or the Chinese Embassy. So, like the waitresses themselves, we simply accepted the situation. Instead of fighting this cruel system we focused our energies on trying to brighten the days of these new-found friends.

Several weeks later the sirens sounded again on the Embassy compound as a whistling rocket flew overhead and exploded across the street from the Embassy. A short time later I heard initial reports that it had blown up the Chinese restaurant!

Images of the waitresses' dead bodies flashed through my head as the dark emotions of life in a war zone began to wash over me again. Desperately I called the restaurant to find out whether the waitresses were okay. No one answered. I tried again: no answer. Finally, after waiting another half-hour, I tried a third time. One of the waitresses picked up.

She told me that they were very shaken but everyone survived because the rocket had narrowly missed them. I breathed a sigh of relief. Then she continued: Instead of hitting the restaurant, the rocket had landed right behind it and killed an American and his Iraqi wife.

Again, that was all I ever heard of the victims. The couple was never discussed again. With the possible exception of the people who actually knew them, they simply disappeared down the memory hole.

When I allowed myself to think about it, I wondered whether our efforts to "not let the terrorists win" weren't actually causing us to lose something else: our humanity.

Life in Baghdad...Stranger than Fiction

June to September 2009

The confinement we felt at the Embassy was just one of many aspects of our highly compartmentalized lifestyle. Families were thousands of miles away. Office work dominated daily life. A rocket attack would throw us into a state of emergency until an all-clear sounded. Then we'd return to what we were doing as if nothing had happened.

While the above may be a good description of the compartments we lived in during the day, it says nothing about the night. The night was when people who were locked into endlessly repetitive routines occasionally got loose from their cages.

Let me begin by saying that the men and women who left comfortable lives back home to serve their country in Iraq deserve high praise. The Embassy's environment was like nothing else, and its stresses were constant and unrelenting. In this environment, otherwise buttoned-down people could do some crazy things simply to break the monotonous and dehumanizing routine.

To appreciate the environment we lived in, a bit more background is needed:

- Due to the dangerous security environment, members of the Embassy couldn't leave it without a buddy, even if we remained within the Green Zone.

  The goal of the buddy system was to reduce the number of kidnappings – a rare but very real threat. I learned this fact from an FBI friend whose full-time job was to locate kidnapped Americans – dead or alive. The buddy system was even encouraged for armored SUVs in the Green Zone in broad daylight. At night, it was a requirement.

- On top of the harsh environment, those of us assigned to Iraq had also accepted a harsh condition of employment: no spouses unless they also worked for the Embassy – a rarity. The separation was brutal for anyone with a significant other.

- Most people serving at the Embassy received three government-paid R&Rs back in the U.S., totaling sixty three days per year. This wise policy recognized the need for breaks from the conflict so employees could reconnect with their families and maintain their morale.

  Unfortunately there was a loophole: the policy didn't apply to assignments of less than a year. My audit team was one of the few groups that was there for only eleven months, meaning that we received just two weeks of vacation. Somehow that one-month difference in tour length meant that we could live with forty-nine fewer vacation days. In other words, we actually worked more days per year than the year-round people!

- A typical day for most of us long-distance married folk consisted of overtime work followed by a late dinner and a lonely walk back to an apartment. After that we'd spend the evening with people back home via the phone or the internet, or entertain ourselves with television or a book. While the Embassy offered some diversions, the choices were limited and largely designed for singles. For those of us accustomed to doing things with family, the "wholesome fun" options were few.

While these living conditions were rough on everyone, they clearly presented more of a challenge to the married folk who were in committed long-term relationships. My initial response – a form of self-imposed cloistering intended to preserve connections to Virginia – was what made the early months so demoralizing. After Herb departed I reached a make-or-break point where I had to either adapt or quit. Fortunately I managed to adapt and navigate my way through the Embassy's strange social environment so that the final months were at least tolerable. Occasionally they could even be fun.

This transformation began when I started escaping my status as a feared and loathed auditor. For months, none of my peers beyond my immediate team wanted to be buddies because my appearance was usually about as welcome as a knock on the door from the IRS. Even during dinner, the Embassy FSOs treated me as if I was doing an audit interview. As a result, I learned to never mention my job unless asked. Once people knew my job title, the conversation was over. The phrase, "Oh. You're an auditor. I'd better not talk with you," was said so frequently that I was starting to wonder what these people were up to. I mean, they really gave the impression that they were trying to hide something!

After trying unsuccessfully to socialize with FSOs, I branched out and started becoming friends with contractors and TCNs (Third Country Nationals).[28] They were a breath of fresh air because they didn't care about my job and would act normally around me. Finally I felt like I was off the leper colony.

One of these individuals was a long-time Embassy resident named TJ. TJ worked as a contractor for the State Department's INL (International Narcotics and Law Enforcement) division. In his former life he had been a professional sniper in the military, with a top reputation for "removing" high value targets. He was a quiet individual who valued his privacy, but he would occasionally open up and share interesting stories once he got to know you.

TJ was the guy who plugged me into the weekend nightlife at Baghdaddy's. Baghdaddy's was the Embassy's only night club, which served as a restaurant called the American Club during the rest of the week. This dining area had come a long way since its early days as a temporary DFAC.

---

28 The term "Third Country National" (TCN) describes an individual hired by a government or government sanctioned contractor who is a citizen of neither the contracting government nor the host country or area of operations. Such individuals were often hired to work on government contracts, or were hires from U.S. Embassies abroad who volunteered to serve at the U.S. Embassy in Baghdad.

By now it had enough style to pass as a disco bar on Thursday and Friday nights – the big nights out in Iraq.

One evening at dinner I asked TJ about the scene at Baghdaddy's. He responded with mock excitement: "It's a *great* place to go...that is...if you're a homosexual!" In other words, the male-female ratio was about 10 to 1, just like the Embassy itself. A few weeks later, I went to Baghdaddy's out of sheer boredom and confirmed TJ's dismal observation.

This lopsided ratio produced a very odd and dysfunctional subculture that permeated the entire Embassy but was on full display at Baghdaddy's. When available women first arrived in Iraq, they usually started off as the polite, friendly, and sociable people they were back home. However after a few weeks they'd realize that they had hundreds of attractive suitors chasing after them. At this point the white gloves came off and they began calling the shots in a unique form of gender politics.

Even women who wouldn't get a second glance back in the States found themselves surrounded by guys who wanted to ask them out. It was amazing to witness the speed at which their personalities adjusted to this new reality.

I will never forget one particular night at Baghdaddy's. While nursing a beer, I observed an obese woman gracelessly pounding the dance floor while a dozen muscular men circled around her competing for her favor. The scene was bizarre – something that would have *never* happened back in the U.S.

There was a saying commonly heard throughout the Embassy: "Life in Baghdad...stranger than fiction." As my stay wore on I realized how true it was, particularly regarding relations between the sexes.

All the male attention gave datable women an incredible sense of control over their relationships. I actually knew women who extended their tours because there was nothing like this waiting for them back home. Let that sink in: they chose to remain in a war zone because the social benefits were so good.

I witnessed another phenomenon caused by all of this male attention: Women presumed that men were always trying to pick them up. While there *were* a lot of men looking for women, it certainly wasn't always the case, so the presumption could create some awkward situations.

One particular case was that of Susan. Susan was an Australian who had worked for the U.S. Embassy in Canberra. To serve both her country and ours she had volunteered to work in Iraq for six-months. Susan was engaging and pleasant but not particularly attractive – not the kind of person who would normally assume that men always had ulterior motives when they were friendly.

I met Susan in the copy room of Annex 1 and immediately noticed her Australian accent. Australia was the home country of an exchange student my parents hosted back in 1984 named Mitch. Mitch fell in love with my sister Heather and became my brother-in-law in 1993. After the wedding, Mitch and Heather moved to Australia, where they still live with their two young daughters.

I had visited Australia several times to see them and loved the place, with its breathtaking scenery and friendly people. Therefore whenever I happened to see Susan I talked about Australia and jokingly tried to improve my fake Australian accent, which she heartily laughed at. In addition, it happened that my wardrobe included several shirts with Australian themes, thanks to my sister, and Susan often saw me wearing them. Also, because I knew that Susan felt far from home, I had started showing her the occasional Australian news clipping that my sister would send.

One day, a mutual friend came to my office and informed me that "Susan thinks you're trying to hit on her."

Yikes! This was never my intention! I thought I was simply enjoying a friendship in a lonely part of the world with someone from a place connected to my family.

This was not just a matter of miscommunication. I had been forewarned by a colleague that anyone accused of harassment in a government job was presumed guilty until proven innocent. Even worse, your career would be over regardless of the official verdict. I was genuinely concerned about what else Susan might be thinking.

After this shot across the bow, I decided that it was time to steer clear of any possible misunderstanding. From then on my relationship with Susan was strictly on a "Hello, how are you?" basis.

Due to the lack of social activities, drinking was a very popular escape for many residents. On most nights I could go outside and see outdoor barbecues that included lots of free-flowing alcohol, with "free" being the operative word. While residents had to pay for the harder stuff, all of our beer was free!

Why the free beer? Because the Army had over-purchased thousands of cases for the 2009 Super Bowl. Here's what happened:

In deference to Sharia law the Army had instituted the infamous General Order Number One, which forbade soldiers in Iraq from drinking while in-theater. However, they retained a one-night reprieve for the Super Bowl as a morale booster.

The over-purchase in itself wasn't a problem. It *became* a problem when the Army realized that General Order Number One prevented them from drinking the excess beer for another year. Soon, shipping containers of the Army's Heineken and Miller Genuine Draft began arriving at the Embassy, which had diplomatic immunity from the General Order. With thousands of beer cases piling up, Baghdaddy's was given the enviable task of draining them as fast as possible.

From then on Baghdaddy's served free beer, but this policy was not enough to solve the problem. There was so much beer that there was no way patrons could consume all of it before it went bad. Therefore the Embassy's social organization began to hand out free cases at every opportunity.

For example, the Embassy's social organization would randomly choose names from the Embassy email directory and broadcast notices telling recipients that they had won a free case of beer and could pick up their prize at the shipping platform behind Baghdaddy's. Richard and I both won a case, which raised an auditing ethics question: were we allowed to accept free beer from an organization that we could potentially audit? Fortunately we overcame this dilemma when we realized that the value of the beer was within the allowable gift amount. I became so used to drinking free Heinekens that one of the most unpleasant readjustments to home was actually having to *pay* for the stuff again.

One day I discovered that beer was not the only thing that was free at the Embassy. When I visited the health unit for an allergy shot, I saw a big box sitting on the front desk. Discretely plastered across its front were two giant words: "FREE CONDOMS." The box must have been emptied over the weekend because Fiona, a medical assistant from Madagascar, was filling it again as I awaited my shot.

With all of the free food, free beer, and free condoms, I began to wonder, "What *else* is free around here?" Then I thought about how kind it was for my Pastor and dear old Aunt Heather to help provide for all of these necessities with their tax dollars.

At least I could tell them that the condoms were a smart investment from the government's perspective. They prevented government workers from getting STDs, which would have led to expensive medical treatments and lost work time, ultimately costing more tax dollars. Once again a tricky moral question was quickly solved when American boots hit the ground.

A related subject, which was widely recognized but rarely discussed, was the level of promiscuity at the Embassy. The constant stress and transience of the conflict zone, combined with the long-term separation from loved ones back home, produced some very strange bedfellows.

To understand this situation, the first thing to know is that all Embassy applicants must get a medical clearance. This clearance certifies that applicants are healthy and therefore free of AIDS and other STDs. This medical clearance was "key" information because it unlocked the door to care-free sex with anyone else who was cleared.

As one might imagine, this key produced a sexual free-for-all that unleashed people's normal inhibitions. While the guys might have been uninhibited anyway, I was surprised by the pervasive promiscuity of datable Embassy women. I'd hear stories from reliable sources about women sleeping with multiple partners each week due to the astronomical male/female ratio. I personally met guys who would openly acknowledge that they were sharing their girlfriends with other guys. These guys, who'd initially fight over a girl, soon realized that, in Baghdad, their mothers were right and they'd have to learn to share. All they could do was lament in bewilderment, "Life in Baghdad...stranger than fiction."

However, as pervasive as this promiscuity was, it was by no means universal. For example, Robin managed to keep a "safety net" around her by spending her spare time working with Chaplains and other Christians on faith-based activities.

Her behavior definitely acted as a powerful filter. If men approached her, they would soon find themselves discussing faith, praying for others, or helping to organize a worship service. Honorable intentions went without saying. From her standpoint, she was in a position to be as choosy as she wanted.

Other women couldn't handle the culture shock of this unleashed environment. While they may have come to Iraq as civilians to serve their country, they never imagined that they'd be confined to this prison of concrete, barbed wire, and guards, which at night could turn into a modern-day Gomorrah. Some were shocked by the lack of boundaries and a few even resigned their posts. There were others who let their lives spin out of control and then limped home for the structure of externally imposed norms. The ones who remained, long-term, were the ones who had the discipline to remain focused on their priorities, whatever they were.

Another interesting social observation I made while nursing free Heinekens at Baghdaddy's was the lack of barroom brawls. Even though the room could be filled with people loaded on free alcohol and carrying guns, I never witnessed or heard of a single bar-room fight.

The simple reason for this was that everyone earned excellent pay, and if an argument ever got physical – even a single push – the party ended immediately. The combatants' next trip would be back to the states where they could start looking for another job.

On more than one occasion I saw two burly men argue and reach the boiling point. However this drama would only lead to a sort of "I'm more macho than you are" stand-off that never amounted to anything. Sure enough, they'd always cool down before fists flew.

This meant there was a certain safety here that I had never experienced before. I suddenly found new confidence around people much bigger than me because I knew that if anyone got aggressive, I didn't have to take their crap. They had too much at stake for me to ever end up eating a knuckle sandwich.

The Embassy Parties

June to August 2009

The Danish Embassy Party

So far, the motives and means for wildness have been revealed. Now for the opportunities:

For months I had heard whispers about mysterious foreign embassy parties – the pool parties of the Danes, the beer blasts of the Italians, and the Jacuzzi parties of the Dutch. However, to attend such a party one had to get on a guest list, and male government auditors didn't have the clout needed for an invitation. Or so I was told.

Up to this point I had spent most weekends at home reading my Quran or watching TV. These activities hardly qualified as recreation and could better be described as Islamic indoctrination. The Arabic news channels screamed "Death to Israel!" while the Iranian news channel brimmed with clerics who gleefully awaited the return of the Mahdi (the twelfth Imam).[29]

29　From http://en.wikipedia.org/wiki/Mahdi : "In Shia eschatology, the Mahdi is the prophesied redeemer of Islam who will stay on Earth for seven, nine or nineteen years before the Day of Judgment and, alongside Jesus, will rid the world of wrongdoing, injustice and tyranny. In Shia Islam, the belief in the Mahdi is a "powerful and central religious idea," and closely related to the Twelfth Imam, Muhammad al-Mahdi, whose return from occultation is deemed analogous with the coming of the Mahdi."

Seeking more enjoyable diversions, I finally resolved to figure out how to get invited to those Embassy parties.

It turned out that I had a friend on the inside: an Italian TCN named Maria who worked at the U.S. Embassy. One day Maria mentioned that the Danish Embassy was having another one of its blow-outs. When she saw my ears prick up she told me she could get me on the list. Wow!

I was thrilled, but then I realized that I didn't know anything about the Danish Embassy. I didn't even know its location, let alone have transportation. So *now* what?

This party was the talk of the entire Green Zone. It even came up at an all-day multi-agency IG (Inspectors General) conference, where I gleaned some vital intelligence.

I had been the only member of my audit team able to attend the conference, and because I didn't have my own vehicle I rode with the SIGIR auditors in their armored SUV. Included in the SIGIR entourage was its number two person, Melanie, who was visiting Iraq from Washington DC. Melanie was an attractive woman in her early forties, and she had recently started working out of a temporary office across from mine.

Melanie had a reputation for being friendly and down-to-earth, which turned out to be true. What I *didn't* anticipate was how flirtatious she was. This caught me off-guard, but for a guy whose romantic life was a distant memory her flirtations were flattering, particularly given her rank. Melanie was high up the government hierarchy and reported regularly to members of Congress. It was kind of exciting.

At the IG conference I discovered that Melanie and some of the other female SIGIR auditors were planning to attend the Danish party. I mentioned that I also intended to go. They seemed a bit surprised because invitations to men were hard to get, but they played along and voiced their approval. Later, as we chatted during a break, I asked whether I could ride along with them to the party.

Suddenly the room got so quiet you could hear a pin drop. No one replied. Eventually Melanie started talking again, but about a completely different subject.

I got the message. For reasons I could only guess, I wasn't part of the gang. However they at least had the decency to tell me that I had to go to

the Danish Embassy beforehand to get my $20 ticket. This was my intro-
duction to the social politics of the Embassy.

As useful as this new information was, it presented an immediate problem: How could I get to the Danish Embassy if I didn't know its location?
I decided to visit the Embassy motor pool and ask for directions. I was so
naïve that it never occurred to me to request a vehicle and driver for recrea-
tional purposes.

The motor pool receptionist said that the Danish Embassy was just a
twenty-minute walk down the road from the NEC's front entrance. My
plan was beginning to come together, but Embassy security policy still
required me to find a buddy to join me for the walk. So the next dilemma
I faced was who to ask.

Richard, my normally healthy seventy-three year old roommate, had
been having problems with his heel that made it difficult for him to walk
long distances. Two days before the party, I sheepishly visited his office and
asked whether he would mind joining me so I could get the ticket. Richard
agreed without hesitation. I felt bad because his heel was really bothering
him, but he knew how isolated I had been feeling and insisted on helping.

We planned to set out on our journey mid-morning. Looking out our
windows we could tell that we were about to face another one of those dust
storms that came out of nowhere and could last for days.

As we left the front entrance, we stepped into another brownish-orange
haze. The sidewalk beneath our feet lay in broken jutting chunks while
garbage, scrap metal, and old tires lined our trail. I now felt extra guilty for
dragging Richard into this mess with his bum heel, and appreciated what
a true friend he was.

In the hazy distance we saw the Danish Compound, which was dwarfed
by our 104-acre walled NEC. Its pale outline resembled a miniature castle,
complete with ramparts made of twelve-foot high T-walls. As we scanned
its walls, looking for a way in, we finally spotted a small sign marked
"ENTRANCE." When we looked up we beheld a ten-foot tall solid steel
door looming in front of us like the gate of a medieval dungeon. On the
lower right, a tiny doorbell hung from the side of a T-wall.

I rang the doorbell and we waited. After standing there for a few minutes, we began to doubt whether anyone had heard us and turned to walk

away. Suddenly there was a loud CREEEAAAK as the massive door slowly opened, revealing a slight Nepalese security contractor carrying an AK-47. In heavily-accented English, he asked, "How may I help you?"

When I explained that we were there to pick up tickets for the party, he asked us to wait again and shut the door. Seconds later a tall blond Scandinavian stepped out and announced that he was the head of security. We explained again that we were there to buy tickets for the party. He receded back into the fortress and soon returned with a long guest list in his hand. He scanned it for my name and then announced, "I don't see your name here... you know, this is a very popular party..."

Now what? Trying not to panic, I launched into a spiel about Maria getting us on the list. He politely scanned it again but reported that she wasn't on the list either.

Feeling thoroughly shot down, I realized that it was time for a different approach. In desperation I went for the schmoozing version of a Hail Mary pass.

I replied, "That's a bit odd," and then switched the subject to a conversation about where he was from. I also dropped the name of a particular Danish diplomat I knew but hadn't seen in a few months.

"Oh yes, so you know Wilhelm. He's been back in Denmark for two months. What was your name again? I don't see a problem with adding your name and a guest to the list. That will be $40."

I handed over the money and in return received two handsomely embossed invitations. Breathing a sigh of relief, I then asked whether there was a quicker way back to the NEC, describing how we had come.

"Oh yeah," he replied, "You took the absolute longest way. Just go out the back door, cross the street, and the back entrance to the NEC is right there."

Our return trip took less than five minutes, much to Richard's hobbling delight.

What a coup. I not only got a ticket, but also got one for a guest! As for Richard, the walk finally convinced him to see a medic about his heel, who quickly restored it to health. I still felt guilty but was consoled by his assurance that our walk had finally gotten him to take care of himself.

So who would be my guest? Some blonde bombshell? A pretty brunette? Not exactly. It was Trey, my gritty Chinese-speaking plumber friend, whose claim to fame was the award he received as the #1 plumber in Oklahoma. I invited him because I thought he would enjoy doing something with a little more clout than fixing broken Embassy pipes. While this party was mostly for diplomats, FSOs, and other higher-ups, he was just as responsible for the NEC's success as anyone else.

The party was scheduled for the evening of Thursday, June 18th. It was the night my life in Baghdad began to change for the better.

I had told Trey about the professional dress-code but, being from Oklahoma, his interpretation was different from what I meant. At the appointed time, he arrived at my door in what looked like a dapper cowboy outfit. Spreading out his arms with obvious pride, he asked, "How do I look?"

It was at this moment that all of those summer days playing cards at the cottage in Canada paid off. I put on my best poker face and said, "You look great!" We were off to the party.

As we exited the back entrance of the NEC we immediately noticed a long line of well-dressed people leading to the Danish Embassy. At the front of this line was a big intoxicated man who was arguing with the Danish security officers. Apparently he had missed the words "professional attire" in large type on the invitation and had arrived in a Tuxedo-print T-shirt. He couldn't understand why they wouldn't let him in.

Ahead of Trey and me was a woman I knew named Jennifer. She was very intelligent and had a wonderful sense of humor, which gave her active interest in politics a sharp wit. During a prior audit she had been the only person in her group willing to help me while everyone else made excuses or disappeared. To top it off, she was also tall, blonde, and attractive.

After we stood there for about fifteen minutes, the Danish Security Officers began to allow us in, six at a time, for a brief orientation. Our first stop was to see the location of the bunkers, just in case mortars started raining down on us during the party. The guide then led us through an outer courtyard and into the main building. From there we passed through an inner courtyard that housed the Embassy's swimming pool.

At the end of the swimming pool was the party, located on the Embassy's back lawn. The setting was beautiful, presenting a manicured carpet of green grass, sculpted bushes, and a garland of date palms. Straddling the pool and lawn was a large wooden deck that was big enough to hold several dance floors. The layout created a calm and pleasant ambiance, as if we were sitting at a Scottsdale, Arizona Tiki bar.

What impressed us most about the Danish Embassy was its sense of order and cleanliness. The chairs, couches, and coolers of beer were all thoughtfully set up at strategic locations. Throughout the night, the Danish RSOs (Regional Security Officers) who hosted the party also stocked the coolers and removed garbage with quiet and almost invisible efficiency.

The party was practically a Who's Who of the Green Zone's diplomatic corps. We saw representatives from the embassies of Italy, Britain, the Netherlands, Poland, Germany, the UN, and others. The Danish Ambassador was also there, making his rounds and warmly greeting as many guests as he could.

As I moved through the crowd I bumped into Melanie from SIGIR, who gave me a big smile and said "Hugh – you made it!" I smiled back and replied that it was great to be here. Then we walked off in different directions.

Trey initially felt unsure of himself, but I encouraged him to socialize with some of the ladies and soon he was fully engaged in a lively conversation. There must have been something about that cowboy outfit because he became the center of attention and was loving every minute of it.

Later that evening I saw Jennifer again. We got into a conversation about politics and discovered that we had similar points of view. Soon we were having a great time, cracking each other up with amusing stories about our upbringings.

After about a half-hour, a big, hairy, intoxicated guy named Marty sat down next to Jennifer and made it clear that he was moving in on her. He also made sure that I knew my presence did not fit into his plans.

Marty was rude and hostile to me from the moment he saw me, which ran counter to my whole intention of having a good time. I decided that I didn't need to get involved with this roughneck and stood to leave, but Jennifer implored with her eyes for me to stay. Apparently Marty had already been pestering her and she wanted me there for protection. I spent most of the evening enduring insult after insult from this drunk, who seemed to think that calling me "four-eyes" was the best way to bully me out of his territory. I thought to myself, "How ridiculous." It was like a high school dance gone bad.

Eventually Marty left and I was able to escape and get back to having fun meeting people. As 2:00 AM approached and the temperature finally dropped to 90 degrees, I decided that it was time to go home. I peeled Trey away from the circle of ladies that had formed around him and we departed from what had been a very enjoyable evening – a long-needed break from the NEC's grind.

———   ▬   ———

A few days later I finished dinner and walked out the back door of the DFAC to head home. Outside this door was a patio where someone had set up tables for people who enjoyed searing heat and sandy dust in their food.

As I walked by one of these tables I glimpsed an attractive-looking girl sitting next to a big hairy guy who was sharing a dessert with her. Then I heard it:

"HUUUUGGGHHH!"

Turning my head, I discovered that it was none other than Marty, the bully from the Danish party, coming back like a bad hangover.

I politely replied, "Hello." But this was not to be the end of our conversation as I had hoped. Instead, Marty jumped up from the table, paced toward me with a determined look in his eye, and told me that he wanted to talk. I braced myself for another round of insults.

Marty got right into my face and growled, "I am so sorry for the way I behaved the other night. I was totally out of line and I hope you can forgive me."

I looked into Marty's eyes and saw an expression of profound remorse. I replied, "No problem Marty" and went my way.

As I continued back to my SDA I contemplated how macho guys *never* apologize for being jerks. I suddenly had new respect for this man who could admit when he made a big mistake.

Over the next few days I learned that Marty was a helicopter gunner for Blackwater. I also found out why he looked like such a wild man: many of the Blackwater contractors grew out their hair to blend in better with the native culture. While it's possible that Marty preferred to look that way anyway, at least he had a business reason for doing it.

I also learned that Marty had earned himself the nickname "Bear Paw." This was actually the nickname for Blackwater, but Marty earned it for himself by inventing an over-used pick-up line. All the ladies knew that, "Once you go Bear Paw, you never go back."

While I'm sure that women rarely forgot Marty's pick-up line, what impressed me was his apology. When I told Jennifer about it, he moved up on her scale as well, from abominable to forgivable.

The Marine House Parties

I soon learned that the foreign embassies were not the only places that knew how to party. The U.S. Marine Guards also had a few to be proud of.

The Marine Guards had their own separate residence, which resembled a giant bomb-resistant frat house. The Marine House was set up with two large bar and dance floor areas, one inside and one outside. In addition, there was a pool table and a 60-inch wide-screen TV in a separate room. On the right side of the outdoor bar was a large sandy area that contained a volleyball court. During parties, it doubled as an overflow area.

I was impressed at how Ambassador Hill attended at least two of these Marine parties and mingled with us common folks while I was there. I was also grateful for his outgoing nature because the parties provided opportunities for me to talk with him. It's not that anything profound was said; the mere fact that he spent time with us was an act of respect that we really appreciated.

At one of these parties I had the unwelcome fortune of bumping into Bear Paw again. I was just standing there minding my own business when suddenly a voice bellowed out:

"HUUUUGGGGHHH!"

Knowing that there was no escape, I went over and said hello.

Bear Paw began with a question that reflected all of the subtlety of Blackwater folk: "So are you banging Jennifer or not?"

I calmly informed Marty that we were friends. He wouldn't let it rest though, and with a weird fascination he drilled me again. "Are you going to tell me or not?"

This time I paused and looked him in the eye. Then I slowly replied, "Friends, Marty. It's important to have friends."

There must have been a little grin on the edge of my mouth when I said this, because all of a sudden I could see the wheels turning in Marty's head as my answer sunk in, giving him a wide-eyed epiphany that drove him even crazier. I just smiled and left to talk with some other people.

But this was not to be the end of the story with Bear Paw. Apparently he had concluded that this nerdy auditor was hooking up with one of the hottest ladies at the Embassy. In his mind I was now a stud!

Several days later, wearing my suit and tie, I headed from my office to the DFAC for lunch. As I stepped from the buffet line, looking for a place to sit, I heard that voice again:

"HUUUUGGGHHH!"

Following the voice with my eyes, I looked over to a table of grimy Blackwater gunners, sitting in their beige jumpsuits. In the middle of the group was Bear Paw, who stood up and insisted that I be his guest at their table. Reluctantly I accepted the invitation and sat down.

There were five other guys there, and it didn't take long for the questions to begin again. They all boiled down to indelicate versions of, "Is Jennifer your girlfriend?"

As before, I calmly replied that Jennifer and I were friends, but then smiled with apparently dramatic effect. This drove the whole table nuts and they began to treat me like some kind of sex-god.

Later I told Jennifer about the Blackwater Boys' constant questioning about our relationship and pretty soon we were both laughing our heads off. Then we devised a plan: she agreed that the next time I had dinner with them she'd come to the table and flirtatiously put her arm around me.

We pulled off our operation the next night without a hitch. The moment Jennifer left the table there was a buzz of excitement, because everyone knew that the jig was up: "YOU ARE HOOKING UP WITH HER!"

I calmly responded, "Now guys, we're just friends." This just tortured them because they couldn't understand why I was getting all the attention and they weren't. That night transformed me from a nerdy auditor into a paragon of manliness, and these guys wanted to have dinner with me whenever I could make it.

After our escapade Jennifer and I became better friends too, and we began having lunch together on a fairly regular basis. There's a kind of safety in Platonic relationships that allows men and women to talk about relationship issues that would otherwise be taboo, and our lunches became a real education for me.

Jennifer gave me some crucial advice that helped Ping and me cope with our long separation. One of her words of wisdom was to not minimize Ping's frustrations back home. If Ping complained about a neighbor who threw trash on our lawn, it could be tempting to respond with talk about the Iraqi neighbors who were throwing rockets onto mine. Jennifer helped me remember that Ping, who works full-time and whose family lives in China, was actually more isolated than I was, alone for months and overwhelmed by an aging home she had neither the time nor the skill to repair.

Strangely, I noticed that after Jennifer and I started spending more time together, other women at the Embassy became friendlier too. It was as if I had gained 20lbs of muscle and lost my receding hairline. Even Trey began to notice. Human nature plays strange tricks.

Through my frequent dinners with the Blackwater Boys, I began to appreciate how much of a breath of fresh air they were. In fact they were some of the funniest and most politically incorrect folks I had ever met. Their whole view of life was different, and there were times when they had me laughing so hard that tears rolled down my face.

It was also gratifying to see that *they* had learned something too: auditors could have a sense of humor! Initially, my jokes surprised them so much that they didn't know how to respond. But soon we had our "We are the World" moment, when we realized that despite our differences we were all just a bunch of dirty old men inside. After that we had a great time together and they helped me laugh off a lot of the Embassy's stress.

The Italian Embassy Party

During my nights at Baghdaddy's I would occasionally see groups of buff olive-skinned people on the dance floor. They reminded me of our Italian neighbors at the cottage in Canada and, sure enough, they turned out to be from the Italian Embassy.

I had also heard about the wild parties that the Italian Embassy sometimes hosted. After all of the fun I had at the Danish party, I thought that this might be the right time to graduate to an Italian one.

One evening at the bar, I struck up a conversation with an Italian named Nunzio. We hit it off right away and in a matter of minutes the opportunity I had been waiting for arrived: Nunzio invited me to be his guest whenever the Italian Embassy had a party.

Several weeks later rumors began swirling like a Baghdad dust storm that a big party was coming to the Italian Embassy. Trey, Jennifer, Fiona (the Malagasy medical assistant from the health unit), and I had decided that it was time to party Italian-style, so we all headed out together. By this time I had learned that everyone requested motor pool rides for social events in the Green Zone, so we used the motor pool to get there.

It was common knowledge that, as women, Jennifer and Fiona would have no problem getting in. Trey had also managed to somehow wangle himself an invitation. When Jennifer asked whether I was on the guest list too, I replied that I wasn't sure but I had some friends there. Little did she know that the fix was in and the list no longer mattered.

As we arrived at the door we saw a tall Italian woman in a low-cut dress acting as the gate-keeper.

"NAME!" She called out.

"Iwanicki!" I answered, knowing that my name wouldn't be on the list.

"NO! Your name's not on the list. You can't come in."

As the others expressed disappointment, I remained calm because I understood how the system actually worked. Instead of leaving, I replied that my friend Nunzio has extended an invitation to me.

By luck, Nunzio walked by the door at just that moment, so I called out, "Nunzio!"

A welcoming voice responded, "My friend, Hugh. Come in…"

I smiled back to the gate-keeper, who ruefully remarked, as she added my name, "Make sure you're on the guest list next time!"

"No problem," I said.

"NAME!" I could hear her call as we disappeared into the Embassy.

As we entered the building I immediately saw that this party was going to be different from the Danish one. It felt as if we had literally walked into the bar scene from Star Wars. I never saw so many different types of people in completely different outfits in my life.

The building that housed the party couldn't possibly have been the Embassy Chancery…or at least I hoped it wasn't. It looked more like a rundown warehouse complex on the East Side of Buffalo. My guess was that it must have been some kind of Annex but even now I don't know for sure.

This time there was no orientation like we had at the Danish party. If rockets began to fall on us, it looked like our chief recourse was going to be prayer. But that wouldn't save many people here!

The warehouse pulsed with hot sweaty bodies due to an absence of air conditioning in the hundred-plus degree heat. Having never been there before, Jennifer had innocently suggested that I wear business casual, so I had selected a long-sleeved heavy polo shirt because the nights could get cool and the Danish Embassy party had been outdoors.

Bad idea! As I roasted, I looked around and saw that most of the guys were wearing shorts and T-shirts, while many of the girls wore almost nothing at all.

Nunzio approached me in the company of some of the other Italians I had met and welcomed me with a big sweaty bear hug. After these kind but humid greetings, I slipped between the pressing bodies to find something to eat.

As I maneuvered I suddenly felt a warm spray raining down from above. Suspecting that this may be someone's urinary idea of a practical joke, I looked up and saw a second floor balcony. On it a young shirtless Italian was swinging a water hose, spraying the patrons of this fine establishment with hydration. I felt sorry for the girls who made the "mistake" of wearing white to this cultural event, though most appeared not to mind. In fact some of them used the dousing as an opportunity to make the most of their translucent condition.

Not exactly enjoying this involuntary shower, I proceeded to the next room, which felt like an oven compared to where I had been. It turned out that my perception was more literal than metaphorical because I was now standing in the kitchen.

On my immediate right was a large brick oven blasting out heat. In front of it stood a muscular sweaty Italian, dripping from every pore of his body and wearing nothing but a thong bathing suit.

This man was the embassy's resident chef and pizza-maker. He was also quite a showman. Pizzas flew with grace as he popped them in and out of the oven for his guests.

It had been a long time since I'd eaten a *real* Italian pizza, so I decided to dodge the sweat and wait for some. He soon pulled a pie out of the oven with his long spatula and I grabbed a slice before any "extra sauce" landed. The pizza was delicious.

While savoring my pizza I looked around and noticed that everyone was just as drenched as I was, even though they hadn't been hosed. In their case the liquid was all sweat. We were squeezed into a tight and barely ventilated dance floor just a few feet from the oven. I was amazed that no one suffocated or collapsed from the heat.

As I looked around, my eyes locked onto a sight I'll never forget: a perfectly proportioned six-foot-six African woman wearing nothing but a see-through lace nothing. I will also never forget the two Romanian girls, one six-foot-two and the other four-foot-ten, who appeared to be glued at the hip. Another appreciative guest told me that the pair attended all of the Embassy parties together and tried to attract as much male attention as possible. I wondered what these women were doing in Iraq and what they did for a living, because they certainly weren't FSOs.

The Italian Embassy Party had been a unique and entertaining cultural experience, but I was hot and tired after a busy week at the office. I decided to call it a night and phoned the motor pool for a ride home, using my government issued cell-phone.

These cell-phones were issued to all government employees for security purposes but everyone used them for social reasons as well. Unfortunately the Asia Cell Iraqi phone company was like everything else in Iraq – unreliable at best. My call dropped at least twice while I tried to arrange for the ride back home. I could only imagine what would happen if there was a real emergency.

The Dutch Embassy Party

With only a month left in Baghdad I actually began to feel twinges of sorrow at the thought of leaving. I had finally found my niche in the social scene and had developed a set of friends after giving up on the clique of FSOs. While many of the FSOs were nice people, they made it clear that they were not going to socialize with an auditor.

I couldn't really blame them either. To them I was an infiltrator who might one day pounce on them after a night of too many free beers and announce, "Everything you said will be held against you in a court of law!"

It turned out that the Blackwater Boys had their own connections with the Embassy parties, so the Foreign Service snub didn't really matter anyway. Though Marty had returned to the U.S., he had introduced me to his gunner mates, and the friendships and party invitations grew from there. That's how relationships worked over there; they were passed on from one person or group to another because everyone was in transition.

One of the guys became an especially good friend. His name was Steve, and he was about the funniest guy I ever met, with a thousand crazy stories that could keep us laughing for hours.

These Blackwater Boys loved to tell tales of their sexual conquests. As I got to know Steve, though, he began to tell a different story – one about a guy who once fell in love and had a child. He had promised his girlfriend that he would stay with her so they could raise a family but she decided to leave him. As Steve described it, "She went psycho on me. She kicked me out of the house and didn't want to have anything to do with me. She wouldn't even let me see my own child!"

Steve never got over this experience, and I could tell that the emotional scars hurt him far more than any physical ones. However there was nothing we could do about it, and the compartmentalized world of the Embassy made it easy to keep those memories pressed down. The best therapy at this point was to have a good time, which was easy when the two of us got together. With senses of humor that complemented each other perfectly, we could cheer up anybody, even ourselves.

Therefore it looked like Steve and I were going to have another fantastic evening when we managed to get on the Dutch Embassy Party's guest list. This was an especially impressive feat because most reservation slots were exclusively for women.

Steve and I had agreed to go to the party from my place, but shortly before the expected time I received a call from him.

"Hugh, I forgot to leave my pistol in my trailer."

This was a problem because Steve's trailer was outside the Embassy on the far end of the Green Zone. "Would you mind if I kept it in your room while we're at the party?"

Foreign embassies had rules, and one of the smarter ones was that guests couldn't bring guns into their compounds. However, because I didn't deal with weapons, I had no idea whether it was okay to park someone else's gun in my SDA. This is the kind of dilemma one encountered when hanging out with Blackwater people.

I paused for a while, contemplating what might happen if I allowed him to store the gun at my place. My room and apartment door would both be locked, so I decided that the risks were minimal and holstered his pistol in my underwear drawer next to my Ralph Lauren boxers.

As we left, Steve mentioned that we would pick up a woman named Petty Officer R*z, nicknamed POR, whom he had met earlier that week. POR was an attractive thin brunette in her mid-twenties with long flowing hair. It struck me as slightly strange that she wore no jewelry or rings. Also, despite her Hispanic name, she didn't look Hispanic at all.

Later that evening I discovered that her boss had been helpful on one of my audits. This meant that I was likely to see her again as a part of the work I did with her boss.

We expected a fourth person to pick us up and drive us, but after waiting for half an hour it was clear this person wasn't going to show. The Dutch Embassy was only a short distance away so we decided to walk instead.

The Dutch gatekeeper greeted us and ushered us into the Embassy. What struck me at the end of the night was that this gatekeeper was the only Dutch national we saw the whole evening. *Everyone* was either an American or a non-Dutch Green Zone Contractor.

To reach the party we followed our escort through a maze of offices. Eventually the passageway opened into a courtyard with a gravel floor and multiple Tiki-style bars. In the middle of the open area were two Jacuzzis, located a few feet to the right of the first dance floor. They were empty when we arrived, but this would soon change.

Steve, POR, and I began the evening by walking over to the bar. Looking around, I saw the auditors from the Government Accountability Office (GAO). I must admit some envy toward these folks, because they managed to defy the social banishment of auditors even better than I did. Somehow they got invited to every social event in town. What really bugged me was that they would *never* tell me what was happening, even though they seemed to know the social calendar of the entire Embassy. Apparently they were auditing something I didn't have access to!

When I returned to Steve and POR it was hard not to notice that the Petty Officer was getting flirtatious with both Steve *and* me. This felt more than a little uncomfortable, especially because we had met only a few hours before. Steve didn't appear to mind, so I slipped away and bumped into Bob, a high school classmate of my cousin George.

Bob and I had a fun time sharing stories of Cousin George's wild parties back home and comparing them to the ones we had here. After that I reflected on how remarkably small the world was, even in a place as remote as the Green Zone. What happens in Vegas may stay in Vegas, but I wouldn't count on it in Baghdad!

The Dutch Embassy had the atmosphere of a frat party, and I felt like celebrating because I was heading home in less than a month. It seemed as if nearly all the guests were intoxicated, so between my celebratory mood and the alcohol content of the collective bloodstream I got into some very strange conversations.

One of my chance encounters was with Judy, a woman in her twenties who previously worked at the U.S. Embassy in Malaysia. After a few minutes she was telling me about her boss's habit of swimming daily at lunch and hanging his wet bathing suit on the office door handle to dry. Apparently this bothered her, but I got a bit wary of where this conversation was going because the Jacuzzi was rollicking right next to us.

As Judy was talking in my left ear about discarded bathing suits, I heard a splashing sound to my right. Turning around, I saw a ruckus in the Jacuzzi where POR was splashing around provocatively with two shirtless local Iraqis. Fortunately her shirt was still on, but it looked like it was clinging for dear life.

Later she returned to Steve and me with clothes dripping and proceeded to flirt until her attention shifted to a new group of muscular gentlemen. As 2:00 AM approached, the dripping Petty Officer reappeared and we all decided that it was time to go home. Lacking a ride, we made the consequential decision to walk back to the NEC.

On the way, Steve and I discovered a few things about POR. As Steve attempted to set up another date she nonchalantly mentioned that she had a husband and three kids. After seeing her flirt and flaunt her wet self all evening, I was shocked at this news but managed to conceal my reaction. On the bright side, at least her story answered my question about her Hispanic name but non-Hispanic look – the name was her husband's!

This experience left me thinking that there must be something in the air here that makes some people forget about their marriage vows, and I hoped it wouldn't drift over to Washington, DC. Steve remained very polite to POR and switched the conversation to his son because he now knew that POR and he had something in common – they were both parents!

Later, as Steve followed me back to disarm my underwear drawer, he told me how disgusted he felt at POR's "forgetfulness." I could tell that he was thinking about his own ex when he said it. Later that week, knowing where POR's boss sat, I stopped by and found the Petty Officer sitting in her cubicle. Her wedding band was on, her hair was pulled back, and her pistol was at her side – a picture of moral and professional rectitude.

A VIP in Town

July 2009

On the day before July 4th, the Embassy Chancery buzzed with activity. Workers cleared the lobby of furniture, erected a platform, set up a podium, and hoisted the Iraqi and American flags. This could mean only one thing: a VIP was coming.

Could it be President Obama? No; the President had tried once, three months earlier, but never got beyond the vicinity of Baghdad International Airport[30] because of a sandstorm. So who could it be?

We got our answer in the early afternoon from an email news release to all Embassy employees. It announced: "Vice-President Biden is coming to the Embassy this evening and will make a speech. All are welcome to attend."

Like clockwork, just as the VP arrived, a Baghdad sandstorm rolled in and grounded all helicopter traffic from the airport to the Embassy. Fortunately "a little sandstorm" wasn't going to stop Mr. Biden, who came anyway by a risky alternate route that took his armored caravan through the Red-Zone. He was going to visit us no matter what.

---

30 *Obama's Iraq Visit: Makes Surprise Visit on Way Home*, Huffington Post 7 April 2009, 29 July 2010. See www.huffingtonpost.com/2009/04/07/obamas-iraq-visit-makes-s_n_183968.html.

Around seven that evening a crowd of several hundred people gathered in the Chancery lobby to see the Vice President. After waiting more than two hours, the drowsy crowd snapped to wakefulness as a hubbub arose in the Chancery entrance. Suddenly our VP appeared.

This was especially exciting for me because I had lived in Delaware for several years. Delaware was so small that nearly every Delawarean had personally met Mr. Biden when he was a Senator – everyone except me. Finally I was going to get my chance, in Baghdad of all places!

Vice-President Biden gave a rousing speech about his appreciation for our efforts at the Embassy. He concluded by announcing that he would stay until everyone who wanted a photo taken with him got one. True to his word, he stayed late into the night to do just that. I still have that photo of us shaking hands hanging on the wall in my office.

The Iraqi Lawyers

July 2009

For obvious security reasons we Embassy staffers rarely ventured into the local community, so encounters with Iraqis were rare. Still, I used every opportunity to talk with them and learn more about their culture.

One such occasion was a lunch in July with three Iraqi lawyers who were advising the Embassy's Rule of Law program. The goal of this program was to support Iraq's effort to establish its new legal institutions.

As we discussed these institutions, one of the advisors derisively mentioned that it was against the law to convert from Islam to any other religion. In fact, such a conversion, called apostasy, was a capital offense, meaning that people who flagrantly apostatized got the death penalty. However, such cases rarely made it through the legal system because a family member or neighbor would usually carry out the penalty without troubling the authorities.

In preparing this memoir I decided to investigate this Iraqi's claim on the Internet and found that two such cases had been reported in the news. In 2003 a taxi driver named Ziwar Muhammad Ismaíil was killed by an acquaintance for converting to Christianity,[31] and in 2010, Hameed

---

31 *Christian convert killed in Iraq*, February 26, 2003, Ekklesia, http://www.ekklesia. co.uk/content/news_syndication/article_2003_02_26_2759.shtml

al-Daraji was shot dead by his own son[32] for the same "crime." While this is not a large number of cases, their existence verified what the lawyers told me. I also realized that the real number of private murders was probably much larger due to the lawlessness of Iraq and the shame of an apostate's family, who would tend to hush up the whole thing.

It also occurred to me that this vigilante-style Islamic justice was very convenient for Iraq's government because it prevented the embarrassment of a public trial before the eyes of Iraq's Western supporters. In gratitude, the government would grant leniency to the murderers.

To enforce the law against apostasy, as well as other Sharia laws favoring Islam, Iraqis carried ID cards that displayed their religious affiliation. The advisor who made the derisive remark subsequently said that he once tried to remove his religion from his ID because he no longer believed in Islam, but the government refused his request. It insisted that, because he was born a Muslim, he had to remain a Muslim on the books. I wondered how many other members of "the world's fastest growing religion" didn't actually believe in it. It was illuminating to see him make these remarks shamelessly in front of the others.

These stories corroborated what I had heard from the MBB Christians and from Michel, our tour guide at St. George's Church. I concluded that, while there may be variations between the Sharias of Iraq and Jordan, the bottom lines were pretty much the same. Heartfelt belief didn't matter. Sharia required the political submission of Muslims, regardless of what individuals actually thought, and apostasy was treated as treason.

This prohibition against apostasy was not a two-way street. While apostasy *from* Islam was a capital offense, converting *to* Islam from another religion was just fine. In fact, doing so offered many legal advantages, such as becoming eligible to serve as a judge on the Supreme Court of Iraq's *new* Constitution.

When I asked the Iraqi lawyers what kind of government Iraq had, they answered in accordance:

"Iraq has an Islamic government."

"Islam controls virtually every aspect of life here."

---

32 *Iraqi son kills father who translated for U.S.*, by Kim Gamel, Associated Press, The Washington Times, June 18, 2010. http://www.washingtontimes.com/news/2010/jun/18/iraqi-son-kills-father-who-translated-us/

They explained that while Iraq may have some Western-style civil laws, the Iraqi Constitution only permitted them when they didn't conflict with Sharia.[33] If a conflict existed between Sharia and a law on the books, the law would have to change.

They also explained that Sharia was not just for Muslims but for everyone. For example, under the secular rule of Saddam Hussein, Christians were allowed to openly trade in pork and alcohol. In the new Iraq, those merchants were under threat of being shut down. As they explained this transformation, Naim's urgent plea for jobs rang in my ears. Sharia also treated non-Muslims differently from Muslims; relegating them to a second-class dhimmi status as receivers of, rather than participants in, Iraq's legislative processes.[34] Again this situation rang a bell, this time reminding me of what I had heard in Jordan.

After learning that Iraq's Constitution declared it to be an Islamic state whose laws must comply with Sharia, I realized something else. The reason these lawyers were all Muslim was that only Muslims had any real say over Iraq's laws. A non-Muslim simply had no authority to say what Iraq's laws should be or how to interpret them. As we talked, the advantages of converting to Islam and not leaving it became all the more clear.

From my trip to the "temporary marriage hotel," I knew that Shiites and Sunnis interpreted Sharia differently. Therefore I asked the lawyers whether there was any difference in how these two sects handled apostasy. They affirmed that the penalty for apostasy was universally DEATH.[35] I concluded that Iraq's Islam-inspired democracy was radically different from what we called democracy in the United States.

---

33 *Iraqi Constitution*, Article 2, Pg. 2. See www.wipo.int/wipolex/en/text.jsp?file_id=230000.
34 From http://en.wikipedia.org/wiki/Dhimmi : "A dhimmi is a non-Muslim...governed in accordance with sharia law...Dhimmi have fewer legal and social rights than Muslims... The major financial disabilities of the dhimmi were the jizya poll tax and the fact dhimmis could not inherit from Muslims...When a case pitched a Muslim against a dhimmi, the word of a Muslim witness nearly always carried more weight than that of a dhimmi... Being forbidden to bear arms, non-Muslims relied on the Muslim authorities for personal safety. Usually these authorities managed to protect dhimmis from violence, but such protection was likely to fail at times of public disorder...(Nearly) All schools of Islamic jurisprudence...treated dhimmi men who married Muslim women as adulterers, for whom the punishment was death by stoning."
35 See http://en.wikipedia.org/wiki/Apostasy_in_Islam.

As we finished lunch I could hear Naim's words echoing again in my head. I remembered how Christians felt more protected under Saddam Hussein's repressive but secular Arab regime than under the new Islamist Constitution that *we* helped create. The question hanging over me as I began to think of home was, "How can a religion that penalizes apostasy with death possibly be reconciled to the freedoms guaranteed by the First Amendment of the U.S. Constitution?"

Honey-Dos and Don'ts

July to August 2009

As July wore on, issues relating to my health, house, and parents escalated to the point of warranting another trip home. After a subtle pestering campaign, I finally convinced my boss to let me add some sick days to my depleted vacation days so that I could visit my personal doctor. With the aid of those doctor visits I was able to go home from July 25th to August 10th.

July's heat in Iraq was like nothing I had ever experienced before. I quickly realized that any weather over 110 degrees was physically painful no matter how low the humidity. At 120 degrees, the air felt like a high-powered hair dryer blowing in my face and eyeballs from a distance of about an inch. The ten-minute walk from the air conditioned office to the air conditioned DFAC for lunch would leave me drenched in perspiration. It was truly hellish. Of course, this discomfort was nothing compared to that of the soldiers in those FOBs who lived in this heat every day for hours at a time. I gave thanks for those men and women whose sacrifice was so much greater than my own.

For the trip home, I donned my forty pounds of PPE gear and waited in the hot sun for a bus to the airport. The next day, the other travelers and I prepared for our connection flight to Kuwait and then home.

Loaded with our PPE and dragging our suitcases, we walked to the paved tarmac and stood in the 125-degree midday heat. We then lined up behind the C-130 cargo plane as its idling turboprops blasted hellfire on us. The 125-degree air felt cool compared to the engine exhaust, which had to be at least 150 degrees when it hit us. We could barely breathe, and our shriveling eyeballs felt like they were being sandpapered by our gritty lids because our tears evaporated before they ever got a chance to moisten anything.

On entering the aircraft the temperature fell back down to 125 F. The interior reeked of jet exhaust mixed with the abundant perspiration of passengers sweating out the local garnishes of garlic, onion, and curry.

After sweltering on the ground in our cargo netting seats for an unusually long time, we realized that something must have gone wrong. We soon discovered that a plane to Jordan had broken down and its passengers were going to join us, which meant that Jordan would become an additional connection. This schedule change caused our plane to arrive very late for our connection at the Ali Al Salem airbase in Kuwait. With no time for a shower, we jumped into a shuttle and sped to Kuwait International Airport to board a direct flight for Washington DC.

Our reeking sweaty hoard must have filled more than half of the seats on that flight. I sympathized with the freshly showered passengers who tried to maintain a respectful distance while crammed next to us in our seats. Thirteen hours later we arrived, safe and stinky, at the U.S. capital.

I had been away from home for six months, giving the honey-do list plenty of time to grow. Despite my jam-packed schedule, it still felt like heaven to be with Ping again. After completing my honey-do's the two of us escaped for a few days to my parents' blissful home on the shore of a small lake in Western New York to help them deal with property issues.

One of those many honey-do's had been to find a plumber to repair a leaking toilet. When we returned from New York in the middle of the night, we opened our front door and discovered water all over the floor. The toilet that the plumber supposedly fixed had been leaking for days and caused thousands of dollars' worth of water damage. Included in the damage were two antique Persian rugs that were gifts from my late grandfather.

The plumbing company denied any responsibility and forced my wife to fight a battle I would have gladly taken on myself except that I *had* to leave. As my wife argued with these shirkers over the phone, I spent the last few hours of my visit preparing to return to Iraq and support the defense of our nation.

The plumbing company obstructed my wife at every turn, using "deny and delay" tactics with a flair that could only come from practice. I wondered whether such companies ever thought about the stress they added to the lives of families already dealing with the disruptions of war.

By now it was August 10th and my time was up. I was fuming at having to say goodbye to Ping under these circumstances, leaving her to deal with our newly warped hardwood floors. Trying to conjure up those feelings of love that we had experienced on our trip to New York, we repressed our fury and distraction over the disaster at home long enough for a goodbye kiss at the airport. Then I boarded my connection flight and took off for Kuwait City.

The Smiling Kuwaitis

August 2009

It was dark when I arrived in Kuwait with the other returning members of the Embassy. Among the shadows and artificial light, large mansions glowed in the darkness. From what I could see there appeared to be a barren lack of plants and trees, compensated by a flourishing abundance of expensive cars.

Shortly after we left the airport we found ourselves in a traffic jam that extended for miles. As we crawled along we saw drivers dart and swerve about recklessly in their elegant vehicles, using the shoulder as an additional lane. In other words, it was typical Middle Eastern driving, but with much more bling.

After checking in at the hotel and ordering dinner, I noticed that every service worker was foreign, mainly Filipino. As an experiment I decided to ask ten of these workers how they liked Kuwait. Not a single one said that they did.

In fact, five of them were adamant: they hated it. According to them the Kuwaitis were disrespectful and rude, and the only reason they worked there was for the money. The other half was silent about the Kuwaitis and only said that they were there for the money. I got the impression that as soon as the oil revenues dried up, there would be a stampede toward the door and Kuwait City would become a ghost town.

After dinner I went window shopping on some of the nearby side-streets, but most of the stores were closed because it was Friday. Populating the otherwise empty streets were tall obese Kuwaiti men in flowing white robes, rubbing their prayer beads as they ambled in no discernible direction. I had heard that many years of unearned oil wealth had nearly extinguished personal industry in Kuwait, and it showed.

I observed that foreign contract labor, mainly Pakistani, Indian and Filipino, performed virtually all manual and other work. When I commented on this to an American I met he told me that this contract labor even included most military positions, except for the high-status role of fighter jet pilot.

The next morning I woke up early with a severe case of jet lag. I was starving but still had to wait a half-hour before the hotel restaurant opened at six. This was a strange experience because I almost never wake up early without a clock, no matter how hungry I am. Flying half-way around the world in a day had left my body very confused.

After breakfast I stepped out to photograph the local scenery. As I walked the grounds, an attendant intercepted me and said that I had to put my camera away because I was near the swimming pool. He explained that the camera represented an unacceptable risk that I might photograph a female Muslim swimming. While this claim seemed ridiculous because the pool hadn't even opened, I returned the camera to my room, put on a bathing suit and T-shirt, and went back out for my stroll.

By 9 am it was a humid 105 degrees and I was already sweating through my shirt, so as soon as the pool opened I jumped in. After cooling off with a refreshing swim I settled into a chaise lounge with the morning's Kuwait Times, an English-language newspaper. Right away I saw two articles about the newly increased fines for criticizing the king or saying anything against Islam. Apparently these were crimes deserving severe punishment. I wondered whether I'd get the $40,000 fine if I opposed Islam's death penalty for apostasy or opposed the king's repression of free speech. Then I realized I was being silly. Of course I would!

That afternoon I asked the hotel concierge what there was to do in Kuwait.

"There's nothing to do here," he replied.

"You mean there's really nothing to do?"

"Well, there's a mall a few blocks away."

"What about the Kuwait Towers?"

"You could do that too," he answered nonchalantly.

Needless to say, I was a bit irritated.

Later I discovered that the concierge had a valid point. "Nothing" was the standard answer most Westerners gave when asked what there was to do in Kuwait. Alcohol was illegal and there was no equivalent to New York City's Times Square or theater district. The concierge had simply told me the answer to the question that most Westerners meant.

To start my tour of the city I braced for the heat, stepped outside, and took a taxi to the Kuwait Towers that famously define Kuwait City's skyline. The Towers stood next to the Persian Gulf, so I took some pictures of them along the sparkling shore. Then, with nothing else to do, I went to Ruby Tuesday for a chocolate milkshake.

That's right; I went to *Ruby Tuesday* for a *chocolate milkshake*! The omnipresence of American culture in the Middle East never ceased to amaze me.

Of course there *were* limits to how far Kuwaitis were willing to Westernize. Milkshakes were apparently too foreign and suspicious to appear on the menu, but fortunately the Filipino wait staff knew exactly what I meant. With sly smiles, they repeated, "Ohhhh...a *chocolate milkshake...!*" and proceeded to bring one out.

The impression of those smiles caused me to notice something about the local Kuwaitis: no one smiled, at least not at me. I guessed that either Kuwait was a living testimony to the motto, "Wealth does not bring happiness," or the natives were barely tolerating me as a necessary evil.

Having chosen a window seat, I sipped the milkshake while gazing out toward the beach. As I watched, some Kuwaiti teenagers approached me from the other side of the glass. They were smiling and waving at me, and I reflected on how nice it was to finally meet some friendly Kuwaitis. So I smiled and waved back.

At that, the teens' expressions transformed into lewd mockery before my eyes. Suddenly they were making obscene sounds, massaging their crotches, blowing kisses in my direction, and sticking out their tongues in a perverted way. I recoiled in disgust and wondered, "What's wrong with these boys?" The female Filipino manager shared my disgust and ran after them, shooing them like flies from a pig roast. She then came back and apologized profusely. I assured her that I understood it was not her fault.

Then it occurred to me that those kids might not even be Kuwaitis. For all I knew, they could have been the children of immigrant workers. So I asked her, "Were those kids Kuwaitis?"

"Yes," she replied with a look of disgust.

After waiting long enough to make sure that I wouldn't see those boys again, I left the restaurant and began to explore the Kuwaiti Towers beach-front. To their credit, the Kuwaitis had built a respectable boardwalk, complete with trees and patches of grass. I enjoyed seeing local families relax together and drink tea along the outdoor beach cafes as smoke gently wafted from communal hookahs.[36]

By this time I was accustomed to the fully covered black-clad women I had first seen in Jordan. These full-length abayas, with only eye-slits for openings, were what most Kuwaiti women wore in the blistering heat. I noticed with resigned amusement a woman with a pair of glasses on the outside of her abaya, struggling to keep them from falling off her nose. I also noticed that, as the abayas walked by, most of them were accessorized with expensive designer purses.

That afternoon I checked out of my $300-per-night hotel room – Kuwait wasn't cheap – and went upstairs to the KBR suite. Among the many services provided by KBR, it also contracted for our government's logistics, and they had rented a suite for government employees to use while traveling into and out of Kuwait. To turn the suite into a rest stop, they had removed the beds and installed about ten La-Z-Boy chairs and two computers linked to the Internet.

The rooms were comfortable, and for good reason: once again we waited for hours because security required flights to leave at unpredictable times. All we knew for sure was that the shuttle for our flight would depart in the middle of the night when everyone would rather be sleeping.

As the plane landed in Baghdad I added Kuwait to my growing list of Middle-Eastern countries I had no desire to see again. What I wanted more than anything else was some DFAC food and the comfort of my SDA bed.

---

36 A hookah is a tobacco pipe of Near Eastern origin with a long, flexible tube by which the smoke is drawn through a jar of water and thus cooled. See www.dictionary.com.

The Water Bomb and Other Bombs

August 2009

It was mid-August and I was back in the 115-degree heat of Baghdad's summer, where the nightly lows averaged between 85 F and 90 F.

The monotony and tension of Embassy life quickly re-asserted itself as I settled back into the now-familiar surroundings. As stark as the Embassy was, I had to admit that it was far better than when I had first arrived.

By now the NEC included two camps for contractors, one on the east end and one on the west. This left sixty seven acres for the main Embassy facilities, which included fourteen main buildings:

- The Chancery
- Two office Annex buildings
- Residences for the Ambassador and DCM (Deputy Chief of Mission)
- The Marine House
- Six SDA resident buildings
- The Recreation Building, which held the American Club, a gymnasium, a fitness facility, a stress-relieving Olympic-size swimming pool, tennis courts, and a mini-food court with eating area

- The DFAC, complete with hundreds of employees ready to serve over a thousand meals per sitting

With construction nearing completion, the NEC operated like a self-contained city. It provided all municipal services, such as power generation, water purification, sewage treatment, fire protection, and regional security. Thousands of armed Peruvian security contractors patrolled the Embassy's perimeter and parts of the Green Zone, 24/7. The Embassy also had its own auto repair shop and teams of plumbers, electricians, and other skilled labor, along with hundreds of cleaning personnel.

For all of its improvements the NEC still offered only one choice for nightclub entertainment: Baghdaddy's. However there *had* been a change to this establishment in recent months. Instead of serving double-duty as the American Club by day and Baghdaddy's on Thursday and Friday nights, it now served triple-duty. Following the disco antics of Friday night, Baghdaddy's became a chapel for Saturday morning worship services – quite a transformation indeed. We wondered whether our congregation would now increase with the aid of hung-over penitents who hadn't been able to find the door.

There was a very positive reason for the chapel's new location. While we may have started out worshipping in a conference room, so many people had joined that we needed more space. With Embassy real estate at a premium, we had to turn to the bar to get a larger room.

Landscaping had also come a long way since my arrival. During my first six months, the Embassy had no landscaping whatsoever – nothing but grayish-brown sand-dirt. It was hard to believe that this had once been a beautiful date palm plantation with thousands of trees gracing the banks of the Tigris.

What had happened? After the American liberation in 2003 the U.S. chose this lovely site for its Embassy. Then government or military officials applied their infinite wisdom and knocked down 99% of the palm trees, leaving a barren moonscape. Years later the restoration of greenery continued to be a slow and painstaking process.

Lying between the Embassy's back wall and the Tigris River was Uday's and Qusay's aqua-blue lagoon, the one I had visited months earlier. While it looked inviting, it was still unusable because it lay in the no-man's land between the Green Zone and the Red Zone. Even so, its refreshing sparkles, along with the Embassy's steadily advancing landscaping, provided a growing sense of normalcy.

Still, we never knew what was going to happen next.

One evening, while preparing to take a shower and wearing only my underwear, I heard a gigantic BOOM! followed by the rush of pressurized water. The apartment's electricity died at once and I found myself groping in total darkness. I stumbled to the closet and found a large flashlight that had been provided by one of the Embassy's many vendors. It didn't work!

My next thought was, "Oh No! A rocket hit the roof and blew up the water storage tanks!" This was not an unreasonable thought because a rocket had landed right behind our apartment only a few days before. Thankfully it didn't explode, because otherwise there would have been casualties that could have included Richard and me.

Fumbling my way to some clothes in the darkness, I put them on and opened the front door. I was glad to see that the hall lights were still working because they shined some light into our apartment.

Next I pounded on Richard's door. Miraculously, he had slept through the whole attack and was irritated by my intrusion. However he instantly came to his senses when he noticed the rush of water and joined me in the kitchen where a torrent was gushing out of the cabinets below the sink.

I told Richard that we had to move his $1,200 Persian rug fast because it lay on the living room floor just inches from the growing pool of water. We saved it just in the nick of time. I then rushed downstairs and found three people in the hallway who asked what the boom was all about. I told them that I had heard it too and that the power in our apartment had gone out. We were all sure that we had been attacked.

I then ran across the common area to the housing office and described the explosion to the night manager. He called the RSO office and reported a possible rocket attack.

Standing next to me was a first-time visitor, checking into the housing office and still dressed in his combat helmet and vest. He was gaping in bewilderment at the ruckus he had walked into, so I paused for a second to welcome him to Baghdad before rushing back to my apartment.

When I opened the door I saw more than an inch of water on our living room floor. Glancing over to my room I could tell that it was nearly as bad.

Instantly I realized that when I thought about Richard's rug I had forgotten about my own. Two of my rugs had already sacrificed themselves by becoming sponges for the sake of the third. I barely managed to get the last one off the ground before the swelling tide reached it.

Then we heard a banging at the door. It was the RSO duty officer, packing a pistol and wielding a large flashlight. He courageously strode into the kitchen, opened the cabinets below the sink, and declared, "Your hose burst." He then turned off the water and everything became very quiet, except for a final "drip, drip, drip."

There had been no rocket or bomb explosion. It had only been a burst hose on a newly installed kitchen sink, courtesy of a Kuwaiti construction company.

An hour later a Kenyan clean-up crew with a Filipino supervisor from PAE[37] arrived with their industrial Shop Vacs. Within minutes they had sucked up the hundreds of gallons that once covered our apartment floor and spread twenty feet down the hallway.

Later, when I told the tale to Trey, he gave a knowing grin as someone well acquainted with this kind of experience. He said that the quality of plumbing supplies in the Middle East was shockingly bad, and hose-bursts were common throughout the brand-new Embassy. The perpetrator was First Kuwaiti General Trading & Contracting Company, which was the same construction company that had installed emergency sprinklers in the residence apartments for fire suppression but neglected to add water pipes. Apparently, First Kuwaiti believed that Allah would miraculously supply water to the sprinklers in case of fire, perhaps like the spring of Zam Zam[38] or something. Either that or they were cutting corners recklessly and without regard for the lives of their clients.

Plumbing deficiencies had been found at over 200 locations in the Embassy. Because of these problems, along with incomplete and undocumented design work and repair charges caused by inadequate quality, the State Department was trying to recover over $130 million in damages from

---

37 Pacific Architects and Engineers: a major government contractor that provided operations and maintenance services at the U.S. Embassy in Baghdad, Iraq.

38 Zam Zam is the spring that allegedly gushed water when infant Ishmael struck his foot against the desert ground near the site of the Kaaba. See http://en.wikipedia.org/wiki/Zamzam_Well.

First Kuwaiti. This was the kind of fraud case that could keep auditors working day and night for a long time.

The next time I heard a BOOM it was not a false alarm.

The day was August 19th. It began like any other, with a morning walk to the Chancery that was witheringly hot. I stepped into the Chancery's refreshing coolness and continued to my office, which was located deep within its massive frame. The Chancery was made of bomb-resistant construction materials and reinforced ballistic glass. It was both solid and soundproof. Helicopters could fly directly overhead and we'd never even know it.

At about 11:00 AM I heard and felt a powerful explosion that shuddered through the whole building. This was not like the rocket attacks I had experienced previously. This was BIG.

My first thought was, "Crap. How many charred and dying bodies is it going to be *this* time?" Reports quickly surfaced that massive truck bombs had exploded at the Iraqi Foreign and Finance Ministry buildings, located just outside the Green Zone. The buildings lay in ruins, with more than a hundred dead and five hundred wounded.[39]

And for what? To prevent democracy from taking root? To destroy the transition from Sunni to Shiite power? To make sure that the United States left in failure rather than success?

Like clockwork, as soon as the bombing report hit the news media, Embassy telephones began ringing off the hooks. Thousands of panicked staff relatives jammed the phone lines trying to contact their loved ones.

An hour later I called my wife to assure her that the Embassy and I were okay. She replied "There was a bombing???!!!"

This was the first time I had ever called her specifically about an attack, so my assurance that things were okay actually told her things were *not* okay. She hadn't even known that anything had happened!

Apparently, word of the attack was just starting to penetrate the states, and what seemed like a flood of phone calls was really just the tip of the

---

39 *Bombings Spark Baghdad's Deadliest Day*, CBS News, August, 19, 2009. See www.cbsnews.com/stories/2009/08/19/world/main5251801.shtml.

iceberg. With the aid of my call to comfort Ping, I turned her into a nervous wreck with news of a serious near-miss.

All the same it was probably better for her to hear about the attack from me first and know that I was safe than for her to hear about it on the news and not know whether I was dead or alive.

Contrasts in Dining Experiences

September 2009

On a more peaceful and explosion-free evening in September I had dinner with a group of peers, including a Turkish friend named Zami. Zami was an employee of the U.S. Embassy in Ankara, Turkey, who had volunteered to serve for a year in Iraq.

If Webster's Dictionary had a definition for "moderate Muslim," Zami's picture would be next to it. She was friendly with everyone and fit right in with the guys. She drank sociably and had a good sense of humor. She appeared Westernized in all respects.

Because of Zami's Turkish background, I mentioned that I had missionary friends serving in Turkey. I told her that they loved her beautiful country and had started several small churches during their stay.

I had barely finished my sentence when Zami's bubbly tone abruptly changed. She reared up from the table and exclaimed, "WHAT? Why would they want to do that? Turkey is a *Muslim* Country!"

"Why not?" I replied, "It's a secular democracy, and foreigners are opening Mosques all over the U.S., so what's the difference?"

"Turkey is 99% Muslim!" she shouted indignantly.

Zami was shocked and offended that these Americans had come to her country and started some small churches. When I replied that even a century ago the Ottoman Empire (which includes present day Turkey) was about 20% Christian, this only aggravated her.[40] I changed the subject to calm the rapidly escalating tension.

Zami is probably the best example of a moderate secular Muslim I had ever met. I was able to keep our relationship friendly but her response to my comments about the missionary couple was revealing. Even *she* believed that Muslims had a right to spread Islam around the world without extending that same right to other religions. The free marketplace of ideas did not seem to fit with her notions of secular democracy, and multiculturalism was apparently only meant for the West.

On another night in September I had an opportunity to dine with Rachael, a delightful FSO in her fifties who had converted from Judaism to Christianity. Rachael was a real people-person, and she cared especially for Muslims. Rachael described how she had shared the Gospel of Jesus with some of them and had actually witnessed conversions to Christianity. "Wow," I thought, "I've shared my faith with only a few Muslims and no one's ever converted."

After dinner Rachael and I left the DFAC and began walking through the calm and starry night toward our apartments. Suddenly there was a low-pitched but very loud siren. Then came The Big Voice, which meant only one thing:

"INCOMING! INCOMING! INCOMING!"

The shock of realizing that rockets were flying toward us was compounded by the darkness: "Damn! Where's a shelter?"

Our training told us to expect between three and ten seconds to find cover. Fortunately there were bright yellow concrete bunkers throughout the compound and we noticed one about ten yards away. I immediately

---

40 From www.answers.com/topic/ottoman-empire-overview: "Until the nineteenth century, when districts with large Christian populations broke away, most Ottoman subjects were Christians of various denominations, usually of the Orthodox church, the descendant of the Byzantine state church. There also were Armenian and Greek Orthodox Catholics, Maronites, and those belonging to smaller Christian denominations; there was as well a diverse but small population of Jews. Within the Ottoman Islamic community, adherents of Sunni Islam slightly out-numbered adherents of Shi'ism. During the nineteenth century, Islam became the predominant religion in the empire, just as Turks became the dominant ethnic group. By 1914, about 83 percent of the population practiced Islam."

switched to high school track mode and sprinted straight to it. Rachael must have once been a sprinter too because she was right next to me every step of the way.

Inside the bunker we found two more unfortunates who had been in the wrong place at the wrong time. Together we listened to The Big Voice repeat, "INCOMING! INCOMING! INCOMING!"

While it was true that hiding in a bunker was better than standing out in the open, it in no way guaranteed our safety. The bunkers were little more than several slabs of concrete that could protect us if a rocket exploded some distance away. If we had a direct hit, the best we could hope for would be a nice obituary.

We knew to crouch low in these situations because a rocket's blast wave traveled up and out after impact. We also kept our mouths open to avoid bursting our ear drums during the pressure change. Our goal was to do whatever we could to improve our odds of surviving with minimal injuries.

After a few suspenseful seconds we heard a BOOM! as the rocket exploded. Then we awaited the all-clear signal for what seemed like an eternity. I listened for the cries of anyone wounded as thoughts rushed through my head: Was there another rocket coming down? Did anyone I know get hit? All we could do was exchange glances behind the concrete as our gaping jaws and crouching legs grew stiff. Delays like this were common because the terrorists often launched multiple rockets in succession.

We never heard the all-clear, but after peeking out and seeing people milling around we asked and were told that it had indeed been given. We wondered whether there was a problem with the speakers at our spot but we never figured it out.

This was the first and only attack that I had ever experienced outside. Rest assured that it was not pleasant. Going forward, I paid far closer attention to the placement of those yellow bunkers.

I must say that I was impressed at how everyone outside, including me, went right back to business as usual after the attack. It was as if we all cooperated to create the illusion that life was normal. Contractors lined up at bus stops, off-duty loungers went back to their beer and cigars, and tennis players resumed their games. Once again we tucked the reality of the hatred aimed at us away and went about our daily lives. It was all just "life in Baghdad...stranger than fiction."

We also adapted to life in Baghdad by recognizing that terrorists had a distinct pattern of attack: they launched most of their rockets a few minutes after their prayers. Therefore a wise person would keep track of the daily prayer times and be extra vigilant outside during those hours. Of course none of this implies that any of us associated these attacks with Islam.

As much as we were able to adapt and create a sense of control over our destinies, we were frequently reminded that this perception was just an illusion. Shortly after the attack, I saw Maria, my friend who had prompted me to go to the Danish Embassy party. I spotted her at the DFAC while having lunch with the Blackwater Boys, her arm covered in gauze. Beneath the gauze was a big ugly gash. When we asked what happened, she explained that she had tripped while running at top speed during the duck and cover alarm and her arm had skidded on a sharp rock, cutting her like a knife.

Several days later I entered the DFAC for lunch and saw the Bishop of Basra's Chaldean Church with an Army Chaplain and his Christian Arab interpreter. I couldn't resist this opportunity to listen in so I invited myself to their table. Looking back, I probably intruded on a discussion that they would have preferred to keep private, but it was fascinating to hear the Bishop discuss his church's activities.

His church was already offering a school and medical clinic to the public. In addition, he was raising funds for a computer literacy program for young Iraqis that specifically reached out to Muslims. Yes, you heard that right: all of these services were specially designed to accommodate Muslims.

When I asked the Bishop whether his church shared the Gospel with Muslims, I got a now-familiar response. His facial expression fell and he shook his head, saying, "No, we're not allowed to witness to them. If a Muslim announces that he wants to convert we won't stop him, but that's the only way." Then he resumed his description of the outreach plans of his church. It was moving to see how this Bishop cared for *all* of Iraq's people, and I felt his commitment to them despite the fact that he was hamstrung.

Souvenirs from Iraq

September 2009

With only a few weeks left in Baghdad and no physical scars to take home yet, I decided that it would be a good time to get some other souvenirs. Ping and I talked about it and decided that some replacements for my grandfather's ruined Persian rugs would be a nice idea.

There were three reputable rug stores in the Green Zone: two at Camp Prosperity and one at Camp Union. With several of us going stateside in the near future, SIGIR's office manager offered to take me and one of the SIGIR auditors on a shopping trip in SIGIR's SUV.

At the first Camp Prosperity rug store, the salesman[41] showed us a dazzling variety of styles and sizes, including coveted silken rugs from the holy city of Qom, Iran. These rugs were incredibly beautiful and soft, living up to their reputation for exceptional quality and fine pastel colors. One of them had a beautiful portrait of the Great Mosque of Mecca on it.

Suddenly, in the middle of his presentation, the salesman stopped, looked at his watch, said "Excuse me," and without further explanation turned his back on us as if we had disappeared. Next he walked to the sales counter, pulled out a prayer rug, and laid it in the middle of the showroom. He then stooped and, with his rear pointing in our general direction,

---

41 Essentially all native salespeople in Iraq are men. Only once did I see an exception.

dropped down on all fours with head to the floor. After that he sat back and, with a rhythmic back and forth motion, began chanting in the middle of the store. We stood agape.

As we gawked, another salesman finally came over and said he would help us. He explained that our original salesman had simply stopped to pray the noon prayer, but we were still confused. If this was the case, then why was he the only one praying?

The whole experience made us uncomfortable, but we didn't want to just walk out on account of it. We continued looking at the rugs with the new salesperson, but the SIGIR office manager whispered that they seemed overpriced. We decided to look through the other stores before buying anything.

The second store had a beautiful display of prayer rugs and, eager to see some up close, I asked to look at them. The representative brought out an armful of rugs with various Persian-style themes and told me they were $15 apiece. After admiring them, I asked whether there were any like the one I had noticed at the first shop, which included a picture of the Great Mosque.

He replied that they don't sell such rugs to American non-Muslims. The salesmen were concerned that Americans would disrespect the rugs by using them as doormats, stepping on the Great Mosque with their shoes. I politely replied that I'd really like to have one and was willing to pay $20 for it.

As soon as those words left my lips, a new voice suddenly came from behind the counter: "I'll sell you my *personal* prayer rug for $20."

This new salesman proceeded to open his duffel bag and bring out a well-worn red prayer rug with an image of the Great Mosque prominently in the center. At one time it had been quite nice, showcasing the Kaaba, with the Great Mosque's porticos and tall minarets behind it.

The first salesman looked visibly disturbed and said, "Please promise us that you won't disrespect this prayer rug." I assured him that I would definitely give it proper respect. This calmed the first salesman down a little and we were able to close the deal.

Our third stop was the rug store at Camp Union, which I should have waited for because it had the best prices of all. Fortunately I still had those two large rugs to purchase for our home.

Our salesman, Muhammad, had a fascinating story to go with the rugs he showed us. He claimed that they were hand-made by the same people who used to make carpets for Saddam Hussein's palaces. He also revealed how we could tell that this was true: they had a distinctive pattern that showed views out of a series of palace windows, each with its own pastoral scene. In one of the windows there stood a domed mosque with two minarets.

As our barefooted salesman presented the rug, he managed to trample all over the little mosque. I concluded that there was apparently no problem with stepping on that one, at least. The designs really were beautiful, so after an exhausting haggling session I managed to purchase the rug, listed for $1300, for $700, along with another one from Iran for $350.

That evening I decided to do some internet research on Islamic prayer practices, trying to figure out what took place at the first rug store. It turned out that Muslims were indeed supposed to pray at five specific times per day. However these times were flexible, and if it was inconvenient to pray at a particular time, it was just fine for a Muslim to make up for it later. In other words, the first salesman had simply given us bad customer service.

The large rug now lays in our living room with its mosque scandalously exposed to shoes, while the Iranian one decorates our foyer. As for the prayer rug, it sits fully respected where no shoe can touch it – in a box in our attic.

Remembering September 11th

September 11, 2009

One day I awoke and was surprised to discover that it was September 11th. What surprised me most was that I had been surprised. In the preceding days not a single soul had mentioned the upcoming anniversary of that world-changing act of war.

On this day in 2001, nineteen Muslim terrorists had launched an unprecedented attack on the United States and murdered almost three thousand people in a single morning:

- In New York City, they destroyed the Twin Towers – symbols of America's economic vitality – by crashing American flight 11 into the North Tower and smashing United flight 175 into the South Tower. 2,202 unsuspecting office workers died that day, along with all 147 airline passengers and 403 of the firefighters and police officers who came to their aid.
- In Washington DC, the attackers severely damaged the Pentagon – headquarters of the U.S. Defense Department – by plowing American flight 77 into its southwest corner. 125 military and civilian personnel were killed, along with all 59 airline passengers.

- On United Flight 93, 40 courageous passengers died when they decided to take down their own hijacked plane, crashing it near Shanksville, Pennsylvania. Because of the passengers' bravery, the terrorists never reached their intended target, believed to have been either the White House or the Capitol.

Over 3,000 children were left without one or both parents. Eight children died.

The dastardliness of this war crime blew away the Japanese sneak attack on Pearl Harbor. In addition to targeting civilians instead of a legitimate military target, the September 11 terrorists killed more people than the December 7 attackers by nearly 50%. In fact it was the single deadliest attack within the United States since the Civil War. It was also the first time in history that our nation's capital had come under direct assault since the war of 1812.

I wondered what the U.S. Embassy might do to commemorate the tragedy of 9/11. Why had there been no mention of any special ceremonies or memorial services in the preceding days?

On arriving to work I found an email, sent that morning, which said there would be a moment of silence to commemorate the attacks. It would take place that afternoon, at the time in the U.S. when the first plane hit the World Trade Center.

At the appointed time, a Marine Guard announced over the intercom, "We will now have a moment of silence in memory of the victims of 9/11." One minute later everyone went back to work. There was no mention of 9/11 for the rest of the day.

This commemoration contrasted sharply with the Embassy's celebration of Gay Pride Day[42] on May 29th. For weeks we received emails and saw numerous posters inviting us to a Gay Pride celebration at the American Club. Even Movie Night Thursdays got more attention than 9/11!

Given that it was unlikely that any of us would have been in Iraq if 9/11 hadn't happened, I wondered why this massacre's commemoration didn't get more attention. Was this just another part of the compartmentalization effort, to "keep the terrorists from winning"? If so, it sure didn't work for me.

---

42 For those who may not be aware, Gay Pride celebrations have become a common workplace phenomenon in recent years. Government agencies such as the State Dept., USAID, and the Dept. of Interior celebrate the month of June as LGBT (Lesbian, Gay, Bisexual, and Transgender) month, and host meetings and presentations on the topic.

The Final Days

September 2009

It was mid-September, and we marked autumn's approach with our first high temperature of less than a hundred degrees: a chilly ninety nine. With my government contract coming to a close, the end was in sight. I couldn't wait to go home.

On September 15th, after finishing the day's work, I left the Chancery office and began my ten-minute walk to the DFAC for dinner. On my way I passed the common area and admired how green it had become. Less admirable was the price tag for that greenery: two and a half million dollars. Here's what happened:

At first the two-acre common area was planted with grass seed and watered with well-water sprinklers. There were just two problems with this lawn care strategy:

1. Baghdad's huge pigeon population immediately devoured all of the grass seed.
2. The well-water had so much salt contamination that after a month the yard looked more like Lot's wife[43] than a green oasis.

---

43 Genesis 19:23-26 (KJV): "The sun was risen upon the earth when Lot entered into Zoar. Then the LORD rained upon Sodom and upon Gomorrah brimstone and fire from

After months of failure, the landscapers finally came to their senses. They shipped in turf from Kuwait and nourished it with fertilizer and fresh water. Low and behold, that little patch of desert finally turned green! Standing around and watching the grass grow turned out to be a surprisingly powerful morale booster.

Beyond the common area I walked past the Recreation Building. Its steadily expanding list of features now included basketball courts, a Pizza Hut, and a Subway Restaurant. With every new day I could feel us moving closer toward an approximation of the comforts of home.

Then I turned right, walked past one of the SDA complexes, and bore left toward the DFAC, noting the "city" of hooches on my right. This complex, called a CHUville, looked like a real city because the units were stacked vertically and had a ring of T-walls surrounding them. This was where the military folk who worked at the Embassy lived.

Once in the DFAC I sat down for a delicious dinner of roast beef and mashed potatoes. Vice-President Biden's visit was ancient history and no other dignitaries worthy of a terrorist attack were present. My final approval for going stateside had arrived and I was already dancing a cakewalk back home in my mind.

Unfortunately the terrorists hadn't gotten the memo that the war was supposed to be winding down. As soon as I bit into my roast beef there was an incredible BOOM! that shook the whole DFAC building.

I thought, "Here we go again!" Except that this time the explosion wasn't just close – it seemed to be right on top of us.

A few seconds later there was another BOOM! – even louder than the first – after which the duck and cover alarm sounded. My appetite disappeared and I suddenly didn't feel very protected by our dining hall's multi-million dollar "bombproof" roof. We had no idea how many more rockets were coming.

The entire DFAC hung in suspended animation for several minutes, waiting to see if the situation was going to get better or a whole lot worse.

Two more massive explosions rattled our bones. This was not good. Even some of the battle-hardened military folks looked concerned.

---

the LORD out of heaven; And he overthrew those cities, and all the plain, and all the inhabitants of the cities, and that which grew upon the ground. But his wife looked back from behind him, and she became a pillar of salt."

While seven may be a holy number for some people, it was apparently four for these terrorists because that's when their fireworks stopped. The all-clear sounded and everyone returned their trays to the Bangladeshi dishwashers, scooped up some ice cream, and went back to work or returned to their SDAs. Business as usual.

The next day we found out that one of the rockets had hit an apartment complex across the river, killing an Iraqi mother and her twelve year old son. These deaths were worse than tragic – they were arbitrary, and served only to underscore the insanity of the combatants, who attacked with weapons they could barely aim.

Reflecting on these events, I realized that it was a testimony to our training, commitment, material support, and over-all planning that these attacks didn't push us over the edge. When I thought about what the folks back home got distressed about, it made me want to laugh. I couldn't wait to get back to those warped hardwood floors!

Going Home

September 2009

At the Embassy, it was traditional for departments to host going-away parties whenever employees finished their tours of duty. These were typically outdoor events with barbecued chicken, hamburgers, hotdogs, and free surplus beer. Of course, no such party would be complete without a roast – of the person leaving, that is. Friends would take turns sharing stories about the guest of honor, expressing their friendship and getting in a last bit of ribbing.

Unfortunately Richard and I *were* our department. We were also leaving on the same day, so there was no one to plan a party for either of us. In fact, given the way some of the other departments saw us, we speculated that the party might start after we left.

Two weeks before we headed home, I decided that if nobody else was going to have a party for us, then I would put one on for Richard. However, knowing that he wouldn't allow me to go through this trouble if he knew about it, I had to surprise him.

While our department had a grand total of two people, Richard's network was much broader because this was his second tour of Iraq. Many of his old coworkers were still there, so I arranged for some of them to get the food and stash it in their apartments. I also asked them to spread the word to his other friends.

September 17th was the date of the event. It was difficult to hide my party supplies because Richard saw me both at work and at home. Fortunately I managed to slip them into a big wheeled trunk that was normally used to ship personal items overseas.

At dinnertime I knocked on Richard's door and we left the SDA together, with me dragging the trunk behind me. To my relief he didn't ask why I brought it, probably because he assumed that it had something to do with our departure.

As we left the SDA I suggested that we take an alternate route to the DFAC. He thought this was a bit peculiar and began to wonder whether this new route had anything to do with my trunk. Just as he started asking, we came to the barbecue grill area where a crowd of about twenty people lay in wait. Suddenly they yelled: "SURPRISE!"

Richard was speechless. He was so surprised that even after the shout he had no clue as to what was happening. It took several seconds for him to realize that all of this commotion was for him. With a big smile expanding over his face, he asked, "Is this party really for me?" It sure was, and so was the roast. We all had a great time.

On September 21st I ate my last lunch at the Embassy DFAC. As I enjoyed my bean and bacon soup – a favorite – I noticed that Ambassador Hill was eating with his staff only two tables away. I couldn't resist one last opportunity to talk with him so I went over and re-introduced myself. Ambassador Hill immediately got up from the table and shook hands in such an open and inviting way that it actually embarrassed me. I had no idea he could convey so much warmth and appreciation.

I told him that I was with the OIG and that this was my last day in Baghdad. I expressed the honor I felt to serve in the Embassy and told him about my concern for the Iraqi Christians who were suffering terribly. He replied that they indeed had a very difficult time in this environment. I apologized for interrupting his lunch and he replied emphatically that no apology was necessary. We shook hands again. I then returned to my table, took my tray to the dishwashers, walked to my office, and cleaned out my desk.

That evening my friends at the Embassy, hailing from Italy, Madagascar, Russia, Malaysia, and even Oklahoma (Trey, that is!), hosted a farewell party for me at the DFAC.

Maria, whose arm now sported a respectable Baghdad tattoo, had decided to put it together and asked me what I would like. I had jokingly told her, "How about a candlelight dinner?" Well, she did it, though the plumber and other partiers, as well as the hundreds of other diners in the DFAC, provided all the ambiance of a candle-lit truck stop.

Mr. Holmes, the famous DFAC Manager whom we all had gotten to know and love, wandered over to ask what the candles and tablecloth were about. When I explained that this was my last day in Iraq, he immediately took out his cell-phone camera and insisted on taking our picture. His combination of humor and professionalism *made* the DFAC the great place it was. In fact, his presence was so important that people could tell when he was away by the quality of the food.

The candlelight dinner and the photo-op with Mr. Holmes capped a perfect evening. I will always remember the friends and fellow travelers that the Embassy brought into my life.

The next day Richard and I shuttled off to the Sully Compound Inn by the Baghdad Airport and then flew to Jordan. Two days later we finally landed in Washington, DC. The relief I felt on seeing my patient loving wife and feeling her rush into my arms was immense. My time in Iraq – the longest eleven months of my life – was finally over. As we drove back to our little patch of paradise in the suburbs of DC, I finally felt safe again...

...except that I didn't.

Bedtime Reading & Nightmares

November 2008 to September 2009

By the end of my stay in Iraq I had developed an appreciation for the phrase, "long hours of boredom punctuated by moments of sheer terror." The upside of this boredom was that it provided plenty of time to read in the evening and contemplate the events of the day.

One of my routines was to spend some time each night reading my copy of the Quran. While my main goal was to understand this pillar of Iraq's culture, I also wanted to determine who was right about Islam's true nature. Was it the academics and apologists who called Islam a religion of peace? Was it my Muslim friends who said that terrorists were extremists? Or was it the terrorists?

As questions arose I dug deeper by reading commentaries on the Quran. I also read the hadiths, which are collections of eye-witness accounts of Muhammad's words and deeds. I mined scores of sources on the Internet, ranging from the University of California's Center for Muslim-Jewish Engagement to Grand Ayatollah al-Sistani's[44] website.

This is what I found after nine months of reading and research:

---

44 Grand Ayatollah of Iraq; the leading religious authority for Iraq's Shiites.

- Despite the Quran's own claims of being clear and easy to understand,[45] it is in fact convoluted and contradictory. Islamic scholars readily admit this.

  The Quran reads like a collection of scraps pasted together almost at random. This is because that's exactly what it is. Years after Muhammad died, the Caliphs who succeeded him assembled the Quran from the memories and scraps retained by his scribes.

- The Quran's 114 chapters (called surahs) are not organized chronologically, sometimes not even within the chapters themselves. Instead the chapters are sorted from longest to shortest, except for the first chapter, which is very short. The Quran's assemblers placed this short chapter first because it was Muhammad's favorite, and he considered it the most important of all.

  As Muhammad Marmaduke Pickthall noted in the introduction to his famous and highly respected translation of the Quran:[46]

  The arrangement is not easy to understand. Revelations of various dates and on different subjects are to be found together in one surah; verses of Madinah revelation {which came after Muhammad established his

---

45 Examples of the many Quranic quotes where it claims that its revelations are clear (there are close to 200 such claims to clarity within the entire Quran):

  1. {2.99} Verily We have revealed unto thee clear tokens, and only miscreants will disbelieve in them.
  2. {2.242} Thus doth Allah Make clear His Signs to you: In order that ye may understand.
  3. {12.1} Alif. Lam. Ra. These are verse of the Scripture that maketh plain.
  4. {12.2} Lo! We have revealed it, a Lecture in Arabic, that ye may understand.
  5. {16.82} But if they turn away, thy duty is only to preach the clear Message.
  6. {24.54} Say: Obey Allah, and obey the Messenger: but if ye turn away, he is only responsible for the duty placed on him and ye for that placed on you. If ye obey him, ye shall be on right guidance. The Messenger's duty is only to preach the clear (Message).
  7. {26.2} These are verses of the Book that makes (things) clear.
  8. {27.1} These are verses of the Qur'an, -a book that makes (things) clear;
  9. {36.69} We have not instructed the (Prophet) in Poetry, nor is it meet for him: this is no less than a Message and a Qur'an making things clear:
  10. {54.17} And We have indeed made the Qur'an easy to understand and remember:
  11. {54.22} But We have indeed made the Qur'an easy to understand and remember:

46 *Glorious Koran,* by Muhammad Marmaduke William Pickthal, Published in London, 1930.

government in Medina} are found in Meccan surahs {composed prior to Muhammad's exodus to Medina}; some of the Madinah surahs, though of late revelation, are placed first and the very early Meccan surahs at the end.

- In addition to being jumbled together, the Quran's verses are also self-contradictory. In some places they preach peace and in others they preach bloodshed. To see examples of these contradictions, read the following verses and see if you can figure out a consistent doctrine:[47]

    [2.62] Those who believe (in the Qur'an), and those who follow the Jewish (scriptures), and the Christians and the Sabians,- any who believe in Allah and the Last Day, and work righteousness, shall have their reward with their Lord; on them shall be no fear, nor shall they grieve.

    [2.256] Let there be no compulsion in religion: Truth stands out clear from Error: whoever rejects evil and believes in Allah hath grasped the most trustworthy hand-hold, that never breaks...

    [9.29] Fight those who believe not in Allah nor the Last Day, nor hold that forbidden which hath been forbidden by Allah and His Messenger, nor acknowledge the religion of Truth, (even if they are) of the People of the Book, until they pay the Jizya with willing submission, and feel themselves subdued.

    [9.30] The Jews call 'Uzair a son of Allah, and the Christians call Christ the son of Allah. That is a saying from their mouth; (in this) they but imitate what the unbelievers of old used to say. Allah's curse be on them: how they are deluded away from the Truth!

- Despite these inconsistencies, the Quran's individual passages always sound like eternal maxims. This is because they speak directly to the reader in the present-tense, with little or no historical context. Therefore it is natural for readers to interpret Quranic commands as living instructions for them to follow today instead of as historical artifacts.

    The active voice of the Quran is quite different from the narratives of the Bible. While some people may claim that the Bible contains commands that are just as bloody as the Quran's, there is

47 *The Holy Qur-an: Text, Translation, and Commentary*, by Yusuf Ali, Published in Lahore, Cairo, & Riyadh, 1934.

an obvious difference between the historical accounts of verses such as Exodus 32:26-27:[48]

So (Moses) stood at the entrance to the camp and said, "Whoever is for the Lord, come to me." And all the Levites rallied to him. Then he said to them, "this is what the Lord, the God of Israel, says: 'Each man strap a sword to his side. Go back and forth through the camp from one end to the other, each killing his brother and friend and neighbor.'"

And the *instructions* of the Quran's verse 4.74:

Let those fight in the cause of Allah, who sell the life of this world for the hereafter. To him who fighteth in the cause of Allah, – whether he is slain or gets victory – Soon shall We give him a reward of great (value).

While the Bible tells history, the Quran issues marching orders.

- Islamic scholars deal with the Quran's contradictions by saying that later verses abrogate (override) earlier verses whenever a conflict occurs. However, because the Quran isn't chronological, it's impossible to know which verses abrogate which unless one consults an Islamic scholar or becomes one. This issue is so important and difficult to understand that an entire "science of abrogation" has arisen among Islamic scholars to figure out which of the verses are valid and which ones are abrogated. Scholarly books such as *Abrogation and the Abrogated in the Quran*,[49] by Ibn al-Arabi al-Maliki, devote themselves to this difficult subject.
- Because this field of study is so unfathomable to non-scholars, the Quran's contradictions give Islamic scholars the power to make the Quran say almost anything they want, depending on what is advantageous. They can proclaim peaceful messages to some audiences and violent messages to others. And because of the scholars' authority over an unfathomable subject, their audiences

---

48 *The NIV Study Bible*, by International Bible Society, Published by The Zondervan Publishing House, 1973.

49 The title of this book, in its original language, is *al-Nasikh wa al-Mansukh fi al-Quran*

tend to accept their pronouncements without question. Given the Quranic verses quoted above, the opportunities for abuse are clear.

- These contradictions in message do *not* mean that the Quran is particularly ambiguous to the Islamic scholars themselves. The science of abrogation has developed sophisticated but clear answers to questions regarding which verses are in force.

- What's fascinating about these answers is that they depend on the societal conditions in which Muslims find themselves. If Muslims are living in a politically weak situation, they should speak in terms of peace, just as Muhammad did when he was a powerless preacher in Mecca. However, when in a position of strength, Muslims should enforce Allah's laws by the sword, just as Muhammad did later when he was the ruler of Medina and Arabia.

- While some passages in the Quran sound admirable and fair, there are many others that clearly served Muhammad's self-interest during his lifetime. They gave him power over others, subjugated women, gratified his lusts,[50] rained destruction on his rivals, and incited warfare and cruelty against non-Muslims.

There are simply too many passages like the ones preceding for the impressions they create to be mere matters of misinterpretation or cherry-picking. I welcome anyone who feels otherwise to investigate Islam's holy scriptures more deeply for themselves.

To get a sense of what I mean, consider the categorized list of Quranic verses below:[51]

---

50 Examples (from Yusuf Ali translation):

[33.50] O Prophet! We have made lawful to thee thy wives to whom thou hast paid their dowers; and those whom thy right hand possesses out of the prisoners of war whom Allah has assigned to thee; and daughters of thy...uncles and aunts, who migrated (from Makka) with thee; and any believing woman who dedicates her soul to the Prophet if the Prophet wishes to wed her; - this only for thee, and not for the Believers (at large)...in order that there should be no difficulty for thee...

[33.51] Thou mayest defer (the turn of) any of them that thou pleasest, and thou mayest receive any thou pleasest: and there is no blame on thee if thou invite one whose (turn) thou hadst set aside...

51 *The Holy Qur-an: Text, Translation, and Commentary*, by Yusuf Ali, Published in Lahore, Cairo, & Riyadh, 1934.

On the treatment of women:

[2.223] Your wives are as a tilth unto you; so approach your tilth when or how ye will; but do some good act for your souls beforehand; and fear Allah.

[2.228] ... And women shall have rights similar to the rights against them, according to what is equitable; but men have a degree (of advantage) over them. And Allah is Exalted in Power, Wise.

[4.3] If ye fear that ye shall not be able to deal justly with the orphans, Marry women of your choice, Two or three or four; but if ye fear that ye shall not be able to deal justly (with them), then only one, or (a captive) that your right hands possess,[52] that will be more suitable, to prevent you from doing injustice.

[4.11] Allah (thus) directs you as regards your Children's (Inheritance): to the male, a portion equal to that of two females...

[4.15] If any of your women are guilty of lewdness, Take the evidence of four (Reliable) witnesses from amongst you against them; and if they testify, confine them to houses until death do claim them, or Allah ordain for them some (other) way.

[4.24] Also (prohibited are) women already married, except those whom your right hands possess...[53]

[4.25] If any of you have not the means wherewith to wed free believing women, they may wed believing girls from among those whom your right hands possess...

[4.34] Men are the protectors and maintainers of women, because Allah has given the one more (strength) than the other... As to those women on whose part ye fear disloyalty and ill-conduct, admonish them (first), (Next), refuse to share their beds, (And last) beat them (lightly); but if they return to obedience, seek not against them Means (of annoyance)...

On warfare and the treatment of non-Muslims or insincere Muslims

---

52 In other words, a slave.
53 ibid.

[4.88] Why should ye be divided into two parties about the Hypocrites?...

[4.89] They but wish that ye should reject Faith, as they do, and thus be on the same footing (as they): But take not friends from their ranks until they flee in the way of Allah (From what is forbidden). But if they turn renegades, seize them and slay them wherever ye find them; and (in any case) take no friends or helpers from their ranks;-

[8.12] ... I will instill terror into the hearts of the Unbelievers: smite ye above their necks and smite all their finger-tips off them.

[8.13] This because they contended against Allah and His Messenger: If any contend against Allah and His Messenger, Allah is strict in punishment.

[8.39] And fight them until persecution is no more, and religion is all for Allah...[54]

[8.65] O Prophet! rouse the Believers to the fight. If there are twenty amongst you, patient and persevering, they will vanquish two hundred: if a hundred, they will vanquish a thousand of the Unbelievers: for these are a people without understanding.

[8.67] It is not for any prophet to have captives until he hath made slaughter in the land. Ye desire the lure of this world and Allah desireth (for you) the Hereafter...[55]

[9.5] But when the forbidden months are past, then fight and slay the Pagans wherever ye find them, and seize them, beleaguer them, and lie in wait for them in every stratagem (of war); but if they repent, and establish regular prayers and practice regular charity, then open the way for them: for Allah is Oft-forgiving, Most Merciful.

[9.38] Ye who believe! What is the matter with you, that, when ye are asked to go forth in the cause of Allah, ye cling heavily to the earth? Do ye prefer the life of this world to the Hereafter? But little is the comfort of this life, as compared with the Hereafter.

---

54 *Glorious Koran,* by Muhammad Marmaduke William Pickthal, Published in London, 1930.
55 ibid.

[9.111] Allah hath purchased of the believers their persons and their goods; for theirs (in return) is the garden (of Paradise): they fight in His cause, and slay and are slain...

[9.123] O ye who believe! Fight the unbelievers who gird you about, and let them find firmness in you: and know that Allah is with those who fear Him.

[48.29] Muhammad is the messenger of Allah; and those who are with him are strong against Unbelievers, (but) compassionate amongst each other...

On lending with interest, which is the beating heart of modern commerce

[2.275] Those who devour usury[56] will not stand except as stand one whom the Evil one by his touch Hath driven to madness. That is because they say: "Trade is like usury," but Allah hath permitted trade and forbidden usury...

[4.161] That they took usury, though they were forbidden; and that they devoured men's substance wrongfully;- we have prepared for those among them who reject faith a grievous punishment..

On keeping oaths (hence, on telling the truth)

[2.225] Allah will not call you to account for thoughtlessness in your oaths, but for the intention in your hearts; and He is Oft-forgiving, Most Forbearing.

[5.89] Allah will not call you to account for what is futile in your oaths, but He will call you to account for your deliberate oaths: for expiation, feed ten indigent persons, on a scale of the average for the food of your families; or clothe them; or give a slave his freedom. If that is beyond your means, fast for three days. That is the expiation for the oaths ye have sworn. But keep to your oaths. Thus doth Allah make clear to you His signs, that ye may be grateful.

---

56 In Islam, usury is considered to be lending at interest, no matter how small the rate. Only zero-interest loans are permitted.

[66.1] O Prophet! Why holdest thou to be forbidden that which Allah has made lawful to thee? Thou seekest to please thy consorts. But Allah is Oft-Forgiving, Most Merciful.

[66.2] Allah has already ordained for you, (O men), the dissolution of your oaths (in some cases): and Allah is your Protector, and He is Full of Knowledge and Wisdom.

I read the Quran repeatedly during my months in Iraq, trying to make sense of its scramble of verses and sorting them both chronologically and by topic. Eventually I reached a point where I had separated the valid from the abrogated and grouped related messages together. Then it happened: one night, I finally saw the picture hidden in this Quranic puzzle. It was as if the pieces fell together and revealed an image that would have been visible immediately if the Quran provided context and chronology or was organized by theme.

What I saw was a manual for conquest and control, whose real purpose was concealed within its jumbled structure. The Quran hides its intentions by including peaceful – but abrogated – verses that Islamic scholars can repeat to infidels but ignore themselves. Thus the Quran lends itself to deception because scholars can manipulate it to send one message to outsiders and quite another to insiders.

As the Quran's puzzle came together, so did the puzzle of my experiences in the Islamic world. When I stepped back and reviewed these experiences as a whole, I saw a hostile house of mirrors where nothing was what it seemed. However I could decode this enigma by studying Muhammad's life and drawing parallels between my own experiences and the conflicts he had with individuals and rival tribes during his rise. Muhammad was a shrewd negotiator and politician, who had a knack for deceiving his opponents and maneuvering them into corners where they could only submit or die. Those who seek to follow his ways use his life as their playbook.

These insights helped me understand why Islamic hostilities, both within the Islamic world and beyond, were so multi-layered and unsolvable. They also explained why our military, peacekeeping, and humanitarian presence in Iraq did not achieve the rapid peace and stability that many first expected.

In a nutshell, it is absurd to think that genuine peace between Islamists[57] and Westerners is possible when the Quran declares non-Muslims to be rebellious enemies of Allah. If the various sects of Islam can't even get along with each other, how can we expect them to get along with us?

Our naive presumptions about the Quran made it possible for us to step into the Islamic world's web of hostilities and deceptions and thoroughly entangle ourselves. In doing so we have also unwittingly drawn fire to ourselves from around the Islamic world. While we may have won quick victories in Iraq with "shock and awe," we may ultimately be shocked and *alarmed* at the long-term effects of our entanglement.

I am no longer blissfully ignorant about Islam. However, as distressing as my awakening has been, it has also informed and empowered me. I have penetrated the ideology within Islam's holy scriptures and it has helped me understand the otherwise incomprehensible problems of the Middle East. I encourage everyone to read the Quran and hadiths for themselves and become more genuinely informed about Islam. The challenge Islam presents is not going to go away, and our ignorance can only cause us to lose a monumental battle of ideas by default.

Please don't take my word for anything. Read the Quran, the hadiths, and their commentaries to see for yourself.

You may also want to consider what some of the West's most renown leaders have said about Islam:

John Quincy Adams:
> In the seventh century of the Christian era, a wandering Arab of the lineage of Hagar, the Egyptian, combining the powers of transcendent genius, with the preternatural energy of a fanatic, and the fraudulent spirit of an impostor, proclaimed himself as a messenger from Heaven, and spread desolation and delusion over an extensive portion of the earth. Adopting from the new Revelation of Jesus, the faith and hope of immortal life, and of future retribution, he humbled it to the dust by adapting all the rewards and sanctions of his religion to the gratification of the sexual passion. He poisoned the sources of human felicity at the fountain, by degrading the condition of the female sex, and the

---

57 A Muslim who views Islam as a complete way of life, rather than as a religion according to the Western definition.

allowance of polygamy; and he declared undistinguishing and exterminating war, as a part of his religion, against all the rest of mankind. THE ESSENCE OF HIS DOCTRINE WAS VIOLENCE AND LUST: TO EXALT THE BRUTAL OVER THE SPIRITUAL PART OF HUMAN NATURE. (sic)

Between these two religions, thus contrasted in their characters, a war of twelve hundred years has already raged. The war is yet flagrant ... While the merciless and dissolute dogmas of the false prophet shall furnish motives to human action, there can never be peace upon earth, and good will towards men. The hand of Ishmael will be against every man, and every man's hand against him. It is, indeed, amongst the mysterious dealings of God, that this delusion should have been suffered for so many ages, and during so many generations of human kind, to prevail over the doctrines of the meek and peaceful and benevolent Jesus. – *page 29:269*

The precept of the Koran is perpetual war against all who deny that Mahomet is the prophet of God. The vanquished may purchase their lives, by the payment of tribute; the victorious may be appeased by a false and delusive promise of peace; and the faithful follower of the prophet, may submit to the imperious necessities of defeat: but the command to propagate the Moslem creed by the sword is always obligatory, when it can be made effective. The commands of the prophet may be performed alike, by fraud, or by force. – *page 29:274*

– *The American Annual Register for the Years 1827-8-9, Published by E. & G.W. Blunt, 1830, capitals in orig.*

Alexis de Tocqueville, author of *Democracy in America*:

I studied the Koran a great deal. I came away from that study with the conviction there have been few religions in the world as deadly to men as that of Muhammad. So far as I can see, it is the principal cause of the decadence so visible today in the Muslim world and, though less absurd than the polytheism of old, its social and political tendencies are in my opinion to be feared, and I therefore regard it as a form of decadence rather than a form of progress in relation to paganism itself.

– *Letter to Arthur de Gobineau, 22 October 1843, reproduced in The Tocqueville Reader: A Life in Letters and Politics, by Olivier Zunz and Alan S. Kahan, p. 229 (Blackwell Publishers Ltd, 2002)*

Winston Churchill:

How dreadful are the curses which Mohammedanism lays on its votaries! Besides the fanatical frenzy, which is as dangerous in a man as hydrophobia (rabies) in a dog, there is this fearful fatalistic apathy. The effects are apparent in many countries. Improvident habits, slovenly systems of agriculture, sluggish methods of commerce, and insecurity of property exist wherever the followers of the Prophet rule or live.

A degraded sensualism deprives this life of its grace and refinement; the next of its dignity and sanctity. The fact that in Mohammedan law every woman must belong to some man as his absolute property, either as a child, a wife, or a concubine, must delay the final extinction of slavery until the faith of Islam has ceased to be a great power among men.

Individual Moslems may show splendid qualities, but the influence of the religion paralyzes the social development of those who follow it.

No stronger retrograde force exists in the world. Far from being moribund, Mohammedanism is a militant and proselytizing faith. It has already spread throughout Central Africa, raising fearless warriors at every step; and were it not that Christianity is sheltered in the strong arms of science, the science against which it had vainly struggled, the civilization of modern Europe might fall, as fell the civilization of ancient Rome.

– *The River War, first edition, Vol. II, pages 248-50 (London: Longmans, Green & Co., 1899).*

Reading these words from over a hundred years ago, one might think that they were the observations of someone commenting on the state of the Islamic world today.

For a modern example of the kind of deceptions that Muslims perpetrate on unsuspecting Westerners, recall Representative Keith Ellison's insistence on being sworn into office on a Quran instead of the Bible. After prevailing in the debate, Mr. Ellison chose to be sworn in on Thomas Jefferson's own personal Quran, which was presented to the public in reverent tones as if Jefferson regarded it with the same respect that he gave his Bible.

The unmentioned facts about Jefferson and his Quran are these:

- In the late 1700s and early 1800s, U.S. merchants were plagued by piracy and enslavement off the shores of the Ottoman Empire's

Barbary States, located in North Africa. Barbary pirates were such a threat to U.S. commerce that they became the primary reason for forming the U.S. Navy in 1794.[58] While a peace was secured through negotiation, it came at the exorbitant price of more than one million dollars per year, amounting to 20% of all U.S. government expenditures in 1800.

Thomas Jefferson and John Adams were members of the delegations that ultimately negotiated this peace, and on March 28, 1786, they gave this report to Congress:[59]

> *We took the liberty to make some inquiries concerning the Grounds of (Barbary) pretensions to make war upon a Nation who had done them no Injury, and observed that we considered all mankind as our Friends who had done us no wrong, nor had given us any provocation. The Ambassador answered us that it was founded on the Laws of their Prophet, that it was written in their Koran, that all nations who should not have acknowledged their authority were sinners, that it was their right and duty to make war upon them wherever they could be found, and to make slaves of all they could take as Prisoners, and that every Musselman who should be slain in Battle was sure to go to Paradise.*

By now Jefferson's motivation for buying a Quran should be obvious: he was trying to understand the warlike ideology of an enemy of the United States.

- Upon Jefferson's inauguration as President in 1801, Yusuf Karamanli, the Pasha of Tripoli, sent him a congratulatory "gift": a demand for $225,000 from Jefferson's new administration. When Jefferson refused, the Pasha declared war on the United States and thus started the First Barbary War.[60] This war concluded in 1805

---

58 *Act to Provide a Naval Armament*, also known as the Naval Act of 1794, from "A Century of Lawmaking for a New Nation: U.S. Congressional Documents and Debates, 1774 – 1875, Statutes at Large, 3rd Congress, 1st Session", Page 350 of 755, Library of Congress

59 *American Peace Commissioners to John Jay*, March 28, 1786, *Thomas Jefferson Papers, Series 1. General Correspondence. 1651-1827*, Library of Congress

60 *Jefferson's War: America's First War on Terror 1801 -1805*, by Joseph Wheelan, 2003, Carroll and Graf Publishers, page 6.

with the first victorious raising of the American flag on foreign soil, in Tripoli, by a force led by the U.S. Marines. This is why the Marines' Hymn begins with, "From the Halls of Montezuma to the shores of Tripoli…"

Using Jefferson's Quran to swear in a U.S. Representative would probably have been regarded by Jefferson as the greatest insult to his legacy that anyone could imagine. Yet this insult to Jefferson and the American public was imposed by Ellison, abetted by a politically correct Congress, and unnoticed by most media outlets. With the aid of a little historical research, I've now seen through the deceptive happy-talk we were fed at the time.

To help you discover the true nature of Islam instead of what apologists say it is, I've compiled a list of suggested books, along with websites that provide them at no cost. Please see *Appendix 1: Suggested Reading* for your own inquiry.

Epilogue

March 2011

When I set out to write this book, one of my goals was to fulfill the promise I had made to Naim, the Iraqi Presbyterian church leader. My plan was to use a portion of the profits to aid the Christians I saw suffering in Iraq. Oddly, in attempting to find a recipient for this aid, I found resistance from an unexpected quarter: an American-based Protestant organization (ABPO) whose mission is to support Iraqi Christians.

My idea was shut down before I even brought it up, which raised a question: Why would this ABPO, dedicated to aiding Christians suffering in Iraq, turn down an offer to raise funds or bring awareness to their cause? The answer turned out to be very illuminating.

While I'm withholding names to avoid embarrassing specific individuals, the actual correspondence I received has to be seen to be believed. In convoluted and carefully parsed language, the organization said that they were unwilling or unable to do anything to relieve the suffering of Iraqi Christians other than pray:

> …We are hesitant to circulate the petition [intended for political leaders, to protest persecution] right now because the recent information from Iraqi church leaders suggests that we pray and work for *all*

Iraqis rather than singling out the Christians. They seem to feel more vulnerable when they become the focus of attention. Please keep us aware of other opportunities to advocate for the peoples of Iraq and the Middle East.

...(The) convener of the ABPO presented an overture on Iraq to the Presbyterian General Assembly last June that was adopted, (which) stated, after consultation with our Iraqi partners, in part: "urge the U.S. government to maintain its commitments to make available sufficient U.S. funds for the repatriation and resettlement of Iraqi refugees and for the postwar reconstruction of Iraq..."

Last month, leaders from all of the major Christian churches in Iraq met in Geneva with the World Council of Churches Central Committee and expressed well their views about their difficult situations living in Iraq at this time.

... We believe that our prayers for Iraq, in partnership with the Iraqi Christians, are a primary, but not the only, response to their suffering.

While this correspondence did not explicitly restrict my actions to prayer, it shot down my petition and suggested no other way to support the Christians in Iraq. I was severely disappointed. Instead of seeking to do anything to aid them, the Presbyterian Church (PCUSA) was lobbying our government for aid to programs that Naim told me would be diverted away from Christians by the Muslim Old Boys' network that controlled the process. Even worse, it was doing this because any special attention given to the Christians of Iraq would only cause them further torment.

Not willing to believe that this correspondence truly represented the views of my denomination, I began my own investigation. I attended several "Interfaith Dialogue" events in my area hosted by various Presbyterian Churches, all designed to introduce Christians to Islam as a peaceful "Abrahamic Faith" similar to our own, which had been as much a victim of terrorism as anyone else. However, at one event, I happened to share a break-out session with the pastor hosting the event, and I made the mistake of asking uncomfortable questions about Sharia and the death penalty for apostasy in her presence. In subsequent correspondence, which involved multiple pastors, I ultimately received this notice from one of the pastors:

Just a quick note. I really understand your passion and commitment to helping the Christians in the Middle East and other Muslim countries. At the same time, I want to highlight for you that our Western antagonism of Islam does not help them. In fact, the Middle East Council of Churches time and again has emphasized the importance of avoiding such actions and attitudes because we do not have any skin in the game. They are the ones living there and aligning them with us in a negative way against Muslims often ends up hurting them. So, regardless of how we feel about Islam, I think it is important to remember that the Christians there would like us to not escalate the tensions. I think our best efforts are in supporting the Christians there and their ministries.

Please look at my comments above as a concern for the safety of the Christians in the Middle East.

"Our antagonism of *them"*??? Also, I didn't see how my actions could make things any worse for the Christians in the Islamic world than they already were, because they are already being bombed, murdered, and harassed out of the Middle East at rates that will extinguish Middle Eastern Christianity in a decade or two. If extermination is the end game, does it really matter whether it takes ten years or twenty?

In the wake of my first real exposure to Islam via *Rumi Returning*, I had learned far more than I had bargained for. My latest discovery was that the same denomination that had brought *Rumi Returning* to my church, along with pro-Islam "Interfaith Dialogues" to other churches, also knew that Iraqi Christians were being targeted for extortion and murder by Islamists, and were being harassed out of their own homeland. Even worse, the denomination's leaders acknowledged that Iraqi Christians were essentially being held hostage in their own country and were so fearful that they dared not even call attention to their plight.

The full impact of this nightmare scenario hit me like a surprise impending death. What disturbed me most was how the truth about Iraqi Christians was silenced by the very knife that was being held to their throats. The Islamists were behaving like ruthless hostage takers and the Presbyterians were behaving like weak bargainers compelled to do the hostage takers' bidding.

The problem of the silenced church is not restricted to my own denomination. Nearly all denominations have been silenced in order to appease potentially violent Muslims.

Probably the most prominent example of a silenced denomination is the Catholic Church:

On September 12, 2006, Pope Benedict XVI gave a lecture in Regensburg, Germany. In it he discussed the words of Byzantine Emperor Manuel II Paleologus during a meeting with his Ottoman besiegers while Constantinople was under attack.

This is what the Pope said:[61]

> (The Emperor) addresses his interlocutor with … "Show me just what Mohammed brought that was new, and there you will find things only evil and inhuman, such as his command to spread by the sword the faith he preached." The emperor, after having expressed himself so forcefully, goes on to explain in detail the reasons why spreading the faith through violence is something unreasonable. Violence is incompatible with the nature of God and the nature of the soul. "God", he says, "is not pleased by blood - and not acting reasonably is contrary to God's nature."

In response to the Pope's words, hundreds of thousands of Muslims around the world arose in fury, burning churches and killing Christians regardless of denomination.

In an effort to quell the outrage, the Pope humbled himself on September 16, 2006 by releasing a declaration that apologized to the Muslims of the world for implying that Muslims were violent:[62]

> As for the opinion of the Byzantine emperor Manuel II Paleologus which he quoted during his Regensburg talk, the Holy Father did not mean, nor does he mean, to make that opinion his own in any way. He simply used it as a means to undertake — in an academic context, and as is evident from a complete and attentive reading of the text — certain reflections on the theme of the relationship

---

61 *The Regensburg Lecture*, by James V. Schall, St. Augustine Press, 2007, p. 133.
62 *Pope apologises to Muslims*, Reuters, September 16, 2006

between religion and violence in general, and to conclude with a clear and radical rejection of the religious motivation for violence, from whatever side it may come. [The Pope] sincerely regrets that certain passages of his address could have sounded offensive to the sensitivities of the Muslim faithful and should have been interpreted in a manner that in no way corresponds to his intentions.

This response was rejected as insufficient by Muslim leaders, with the Muslim Brotherhood declaring, "Has he presented a personal apology for statements by which he clearly is convinced? No."[63]

As churches continued to burn and Christians continued to be attacked, the Pope humbled himself further by issuing a deeper apology the next day:[64]

At this time, I wish also to add that I am deeply sorry for the reactions in some countries to a few passages of my address at the University of Regensburg, which were considered offensive to the sensibility of Muslims. These in fact were a quotation from a medieval text, which do not in any way express my personal thought.

Of course nearly all of the news coverage of this disaster blamed the Pope for stirring up Muslim anger. Essentially none of the reporters noticed that the violent Muslim response validated the Pope's quotation. They also failed to recognize the ruthless victory of power over reason when Muslim violence forced the Pope to apologize for calling attention to Muslim violence.

For the remainder of his papacy, Pope Benedict XVI remained virtually silent about Islam, despite continued attacks on Catholics by Muslim terrorists, including:

- The January 2008 murder of Philippine Priest Reynaldo Jesus Roda by a gang of 10 Muslim gunmen who tried to kidnap him while he was praying in his chapel[65]

---

63 *Pope Statement Not Enough – Muslim Brotherhood*, Reuters, September 16, 2006
64 *The Regensburg Speech of Pope Benedict XVI*, Islam Today, September 18, 2006, http://en.islamtoday.net/artshow-416-2998.htm
65 *Oblate of Mary Immaculate priest gunned down in a kidnapping attempt in the southern Philippines*, by Santosh Digal, January 15, 2008, Asia News, http://www.asianews.it/index.php?l=en&art=11260

- The February 2008 terrorist kidnapping and subsequent murder of Iraqi Archbishop Paulos Faraj Rahho[66]
- The June 2010 decapitation of Turkey's Archbishop Luigi Padovese by his Muslim driver[67]
- The October 31, 2010 terrorist massacre at the Our Lady of Salvation Cathedral in Baghdad, Iraq, which killed 58 worshippers during a Sunday evening mass[68]
- The February 2011 near-decapitation of Tunisian Priest Marek Marius Rybinski[69]

This level of restraint is remarkable, given:

- The July 1998 terrorist murders by automatic gunfire of three nuns in Yemen[70]
- The terrorist murder of Philippine Bishop Benjamin D. de Jesus in 1997 outside of his cathedral[71]
- The attempted assassination of Pope John Paul II in 1981 by Mehmet Ali Ağca, a Turkish Muslim[72]

These are only some of the most prominent attacks, and only within the Catholic Church. A survey of all of the church burnings and murders of Christian leaders and laity would require another book much thicker than this one.

---

66 *Death comes for an Iraqi Archbishop*, by Jeff Israely, March 13, 2008, Time Magazine, http://www.time.com/time/world/article/0,8599,1722317,00.html

67 *Catholic Bishop Luigi Padovese Assassinated in Southern Turkey*, by Geries Othman, June 4, 2010, Asia News, http://www.catholic.org/international/international_story.php?id=36811

68 *Church Attack Seen as Strike at Iraq's Core*, by Anthony Shadid, November 1, 2010, The New York Times, http://www.nytimes.com/2010/11/02/world/middleeast/02iraq.html?adxnnl=1&adxnnlx=1311895722-nuQalJU/JQvt5wF0KJtQdA

69 *TUNISIA: Polish priest slain amid rising Islamic militancy*, by Carol J. Williams, February 18, 2011, The Los Angeles Times, http://latimesblogs.latimes.com/babylonbeyond/2011/02/tunisia-protest.html

70 *Three nuns shot dead in Yemen*, BBC News, July 27, 1998, http://news.bbc.co.uk/2/hi/middle_east/140424.stm

71 *Grenade explodes outside Sulu Catholic church*, The Mindanao Examiner, January 10, 2010, http://mindanaoexaminer.com/news.php?news_id=20100109210929

72 *Man Who Shot Pope in 1981 Is Freed*, By Sebnem Arsu, January 18, 2010, New York Times, http://www.nytimes.com/2010/01/19/world/europe/19pope.html

Clearly these are not simply the random actions of isolated lunatics. Extreme as they were, all of these attacks found their roots in Islamic doctrine.

The journey of discovery launched by *Rumi Returning* has taken me many places, but the scenes I remember most are those of the Christian communities in Iraq so terrorized that they couldn't even scream. Now that I am back in the United States, I find that I see familiar events in a whole new way, such as Churches hosting interfaith events with Mosques... while their denominations are paralyzed by fear for their Iraqi parishioners. Meanwhile, the "Arab Spring" has only escalated violence against Christians in other Islamic countries such as Egypt, Libya, Syria, and Algeria.

Throughout the Islamic world, Christians are increasingly finding that they are hostages in their own homelands. If you believe that this is the way things should be, please join in the conspiracy of silence.

On the other hand, if you are shocked and alarmed by what you have read, please don't close your eyes again. Tell others about this dire situation and start discussing what can be done about it.

If you are active in politics, educate your legislators and demand that funds be withheld from countries that tolerate or endorse religious persecution.

If you are active in a church, discuss persecuted Christians at church meetings and find out what your denomination is doing for them. Submit prayer requests for persecuted Christians to your prayer chains.

You may also want to donate your time and treasure to aid non-Muslims suffering in the Islamic world. To this end, please consider supporting organizations such as the ones listed in *Appendix 2: How You Can Help*.

Regardless of what you choose to do, please always remember the torment being suffered by non-Muslims in Muslim lands. Their silence is their greatest cry for help.

Appendix 1

Suggested Reading

While all of the books below are available in hardcopy, they can also be found on-line at no cost. Each title is followed by a link to a free version of its text, with the caveat that the links may change or be removed by their hosts. If a link fails, enter the book's title into a search engine. You are almost certain to find a new URL for the same book somewhere else on the web.

- Quran (three different translations)
  www.usc.edu/org/cmje/religious-texts/quran/
- Hadith (four of the most authoritative compilations)
  http://www.usc.edu/org/cmje/religious-texts/hadith/
- The Life of Muhammad, by Ibn Ishak
  http://www.archive.org/stream/Sirat-lifeOfMuhammadBy-ibnIshaq/SiratIbnIahaqInEnglish#page/n0/mode/2up
- The Reliance of the Traveller (A classical manual of Islamic sacred law) http://www.shafiifiqh.com/maktabah/relianceoftraveller.pdf
- Towards Understanding the Quran, by Syed Abul Ala Maududi (commentary) http://www.islamicstudies.info/tafheem.php

- Islamic Laws of Iraqi Grand Ayatollah Ali al-Sistani
  Home Page: www.sistani.org/index.php?p=251364&id=48
  This website discusses some fascinating aspects of Sharia. Read
  the following pages to learn how al-Sistani instructs Muslims
  regarding:

  - Infidels:
    www.sistani.org/index.php?p=251364&id=48&pid=2132
  - Spoils of war:
    www.sistani.org/index.php?p=251364&id=48&pid=2291
  - Apostasy:
    www.sistani.org/index.php?p=251364&id=48&pid=2352
  - Pre-pubescent marriage:
    www.sistani.org/index.php?p=251364&id=48&pid=2348
  - Marriage without the consent of the woman:
    www.sistani.org/index.php?p=251364&id=48&pid=2346
  - The requirement that wives be sexually available to
    husbands at all times:
    www.sistani.org/index.php?p=251364&id=48&pid=2349
  - Temporary marriage (=pleasure marriage):
    www.sistani.org/index.php?p=251364&id=48&pid=2350

- The Concept of Crime in the Afghan Criminal Justice System:
  The Paradox between Secular, Tradition and Islamic Law, by
  Ahmed Hamdy Tawfik, Presiding Judge, Ministry of Justice,
  Cairo, Egypt Judicial Affairs Officer, United Nations Assistance
  Mission in Afghanistan (UNAMA)
  http://et-lawfirm.com/publications.html.html
  NOTE: Read the sections entitled *2. Apostasy* and *3. Adultery and
  Rape*

Appendix 2

How You Can Help

Thankfully there are organizations willing to speak-out in support of the Iraqi Christians and come to their aid. Listed below are some but certainly not all of the organizations you may wish to support. Each website provides valuable information on their activities and offers a free newsletter that you can sign up for:

Barnabas Fund	www.barnabasfund.org	Mission: Support Christians where they are in a minority and suffer discrimination, oppression & persecution as a consequence of their faith.
Catholics Aid to the Church in Need	www.churchinneed.org	Mission: Defend the persecuted Church. Their foremost task is to stand by those who suffer violence & repression for sake of their Catholic faith, although no viable & appropriate request on behalf of a persecuted Church will go unanswered.

Christian Freedom International	www.christianfreedom.org	Misson: Have relationships with indigenous believers and churches, working together to provide medicine, safe-houses, aid, Bibles, education, micro-enterprise, documentation, and advocacy to Christians and their families who are on the front lines of persecution.
Christian Solidarity International	http://csi-usa.org	Mission: Campaign for religious liberty and human dignity, and assist victims of religious persecution, victimized children and victims of catastrophe.
International Christian Concern	www.persecution.org	Mission: Serve and build the persecuted Church in strength and breadth through effective Advocacy (government lobbying), Assistance (practical help), and Awareness (news reports and press releases).
International Christian Response	www.christianresponse.org	Mission: Provide spiritual and material assistance that enables persecuted Christians to proclaim the Gospel and plant churches in hostile countries.
Open Doors	www.opendoorsusa.org	Mission: Serve Persecuted Christians Worldwide; Strengthen persecuted believers worldwide through community development, Bible & literature distribution, leadership training & education and ministries of prayer and advocacy.

Release International	www.releaseinterna-tional.org	Mission: Serve the persecuted church around the world in five key ways: 1. Showing God's compassion: Providing for the needs of the families of martyrs and prisoners 2. Serving God's church: Enabling them to survive persecution and its effects 3. Sharing God's love: Helping the persecuted church win to Christ those who are opposed to the Gospel 4. Spreading God's Word: Supplying Bibles and literature to meet the need for growth and evangelism 5. Speaking as God's advocates: Being the voice of the martyrs and the oppressed
Voice of the Martyrs	www.persecution.com	Mission: Serve the persecuted church through practical and spiritual assistance while leading Christians in the free world into fellowship with them.

Made in the USA
Middletown, DE
18 September 2022

10717943R00116